Series / Number 02-018

Urbanization in a Developing Economy: Indian Perspectives and Patterns

DEBNATH MOOKHERJEE
Western Washington State College

RICHARD L. MORRILL
University of Washington

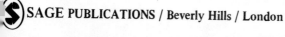 SAGE PUBLICATIONS / Beverly Hills / London

For information address:

SAGE PUBLICATIONS, INC.
275 South Beverly Drive
Beverly Hills, California 90212

SAGE PUBLICATIONS, INC.
St George's House / 44 Hatton Garden
London EC1N 8ER

International Standard Book Number 0-8039-0300-6

Library of Congress Catalog Card No. L.C. 73-86707

FIRST PRINTING

When citing a professional paper, please use the proper form. Remember to cite the
correct Sage Professional Paper series title and include the paper number. One of the
two following formats can be adapted (depending on the style manual used):

(1) AZAR, E. E. (1972) "International Events Interaction Analysis." Sage
Professional Paper in International Studies, 1, 02-001. Beverly Hills and London:
Sage Pubns.

OR

(2) Azar, Edward E. 1972. *International Events Interaction Analysis.* Sage
Professional Paper in International Studies, Vol. 1., no. 02-001. Beverly Hills and
London: Sage Publications.

CONTENTS

LIST OF FIGURES AND TABLES

Urbanization in a Developing Economy: Indian Perspectives and Patterns

DEBNATH MOOKHERJEE
Western Washington State College

RICHARD L. MORRILL
University of Washington

INTRODUCTION

The purpose of this monograph is to provide some insights into the complex process of urbanization. Although the frame of reference of this urbanization phenomenon embraces a wide range of topics, we have been necessarily selective in discussing them in context of a single developing country, India. The final outcome of our effort, therefore, should not be construed as being applicable to all developing nations. However, the patterns and perspectives that have emerged we believe to be of relevance in promoting an understanding of the urbanization characteristics of many of the developing nations currently facing the multitudinous problems of urban growth and challenges of socioeconomic planning similar to that of India's.

Within the roughly two decades since the beginning of centrally planned economic development in India and China, virtually every village and every rural area has felt the impact of growing urbanization, directly or indirectly. The end of Colonialism and the

AUTHOR'S NOTE: *On behalf of my co-author and myself, I wish to thank Eugene Hoerauf, cartographer, for shaping the maps and illustrations, and Mrs. Jane Clark of the Bureau for Faculty Research for typing the manuscript—both of Western Washington State College. Thanks are also due to Miss Virginia Hetrick, a graduate student in geography at the University of Washington and David Schoen, the former cartographer at Western for their help in processing some of the data in the initial* coming of national independence in India [has] sparked a sustained drive to lift the country out of its relative poverty, compounded by population growth, and impel it into abundance [Murphy, 1972: 250].

However, in the wake of a massive rise in the total and urban population, the strain of this drive has multiplied and the goal has assumed almost a mirage quality. In view of the multitude of problems to a large extent stemming from and engulfing the urban areas, this dramatic increase of population in cities in most of the developing countries, termed the "new urbanization," is considered to be of special importance. A graphic account of this dismal picture is presented by Barbara Ward, who following her analogy of urbanization as a "transmission belt from old to new," suggests that

in the developing continents in the late twentieth century the transmission belt is not working, or rather it is working erratically and dangerously. It is pouring the new migrant multitudes not into a potentially viable urban order but into an urban wilderness where opportunities grow less as the millions pile on top of one another and the farms do not feed them or the industries employ them [1969: 62].

Although India's urban population is less than one-fifth of her total population, there is some consensus among social scientists that the current state of demographic and economic conditions are generally not conducive to further growth in their present form. As a result of the high natural increase of population and the massive migration to cities which are the nation's centers for economic growth and social change, study of the problems and prospects of urbanization and urban-industrial development has become an urgent task. From the alleviation of existing physical congestion, housing, unemployment, and the like, to the formulation of national policies on the distribution of urban population and economic activities, this urgency is indicated by quickening interest in the study of the urban environment from a wide range of perspectives. As the beneficiaries of a plethora of recent publications in the field of Indian urban affairs, possibly indicative of the gamut of complex urban

phase of the analysis. To Dr. James Scott, our colleague at Western, who read an earlier draft of the manuscript and offered many editorial comments and suggestions, we express our sincere appreciation.

It seems too formal to express my thankfulness to my wife Supriya, who shared my involvement in the project and provided assistance and important criticism throughout the study. [Debnath Mookherjee] conditions, our knowledge is being enriched with studies concerning patterns of small towns; we have gained information on a variety of problems of larger cities of national importance; and we have a dawning awareness of regional differences in urban characteristics and patterns. However, our understanding of the complex processes leading to urbanization in the subcontinent is far from complete.

Until recently there have been very few systematic research studies concerning India's urban and developmental patterns,[1] and methodological studies aimed at explanation and understanding of nationwide urban processes are yet to come. The need for an "integrative theoretical framework" for analytical studies on the underdeveloped world has been voiced by concerned scholars (Jacobson and Prakash, 1971: 16; Burton, 1969: 165-166), and the necessity of empirical research, "an important (though not invariable) component of theory," has already been acknowledged (Burton, 1969: 149; Colm and Geiger, 1962: 66). However, the applicability of theories and models developed and tested in the western world to underdeveloped societies elsewhere has been questioned in recent years. Burton (1969: 150), for example, has observed: "Recent experience in India permits an exploration of some of the pitfalls of exporting western planning methods to alien cultures and underscores the need for more firmly grounded theoretical models of nonwestern societies." It is increasingly realized that the effectiveness of any urban-industrial plan or policy for the developing nations will be difficult, if not impossible to achieve, without systematic assessment of forces leading to urban and industrial development in its particular political, socioeconomic, or geographic context. As Jacobson and Prakash (1971: 18) have stated, "Within the framework of whatever general theory may emerge, there exist significant inter-regional and intra-regional differences that must be taken into account in the formulation of policy."

The present research paper does not claim to fill this need, rather it proposes to take an exploratory step towards this goal. Our emphasis is on a systematic analysis of urban-industrial processes and patterns of India in order to portray some empirical insights. The post-independence period in India has witnessed a tremendous effort to develop the country, with heightened attention being given in recent years to the deconcentration and dispersal of industries as a means of alleviating the urban and economic imbalances within the nation.

Against this backdrop, it is considered worthwhile to assess the association of certain occupational, demographic, and developmental factors with urban growth and urbanization. In the first part, we present an overview of the urban concept and some of the pertinent issues in urban-industrial relationships, preceding a brief discussion of the contemporary situation in India. In the second, we seek to assess the relationship of selected variables with urbanization and urban growth in different states and among various urban size groups by the use of multiple regression models. Nonavailability of certain data which are considered to be of importance—for example, detailed information on urban migration and natural increase—has severely curtailed the scope of the present study. However, in spite of this limitation we have been ambitious enough to point out certain tendencies concerning urbanization in India which, we believe, will at least be of some heuristic value and will contribute toward a greater understanding of urbanization in a developing economy such as that of India.

URBAN AND INDUSTRIAL DEVELOPMENT

THE URBAN CONCEPT

Agreement on the meaning of the term "urban" is basic to any qualitative or quantitative assessment or evaluation of the pattern of urbanization. Although in recent years the literature has been enriched by numerous contributions on various aspects and concepts of urbanization, social scientists have not yet reached a satisfactory conclusion on the definition of an urban place. The concept of "urban" differs not only from one nation to another, but also within regions of the same nation (Glass, 1964: 4), thus rendering the task of assessment and comparison of the urbanization processes and urban patterns in the national and regional contexts more difficult.

However, the concept of an urban settlement—be it called a city, town, or place—usually presupposes an environment different from that of the surrounding rural area or countryside. The characterization of such an environment is based on a wide range of demographic, cultural, and political criteria; and in defining urban areas, nations have adopted various combinations of such criteria to recognize the urban environment. Based on a survey of the censuses of 52 countries, the United Nations has identified five major concepts among those used in defining urban areas: administrative areas, population size, local government areas, urban characteristics, and predominant economic activities (Chandrasekaran and Zachariah, 1964: 52-53). Criteria similar to all but the first of the above have been utilized in the census definition of urban places in India.

Although basically an agrarian country, urban ways of life are not new in India. Historical evidence shows that in early ages India developed well-planned cities, such as Ayodhya, Indraprastha, Pataliputra, Tamralipti, and many others, which "provided the necessary amenities for urban living," even though urban living under a weak technology was far removed from what appears to be urbanism today. Contemporary urban life has become more complex, urban-centered activities having assumed major roles in shaping the developmental goals for the people in most presently developing nations. This change requires a clear identification of urban places based on factors relevant in the Indian context—factors which may account for the function, size, hierarchy, and various other social and physical characteristics that shape the form and structure of places. Such an identification would not only have the potential to indicate present patterns and problems, but also to provide necessary guidelines for proper assessment of the role of urbanization in the future development of the country.

The *Census of India*, a major source of information on the concepts and definition of the term "urban" and on the trend of urbanization, has published "tests for eligibility" for places to be considered as urban since 1881. Up to the 1961 census, the definition of "urban" had been modified or changed in each census.[2] Due to the diverse conditions prevailing in the political units in India, adherence to a strict operational framework for assessment of urban places was not always possible (*Census of India, 1961*, 1964a: 51) thus creating problems in regards to comparability of the measures of urbanization. In 1961, in recognition of this problem, the Census Commission adopted a rather rigid definition to be followed throughout the country: to be considered "urban," a place should be either a "municipal corporation or a municipal area," or should be under a town committee or a notified area committee or a cantonment board. In the absence of "any statutory label of administration," other places may qualify as urban on the basis of certain criteria, such as: (a) a density of not less than 1,000 inhabitants per square mile; (b) a minimum population of 5,000; (c) three-fourths of the working population occupied outside of agriculture; and (d) any other place which, according to the Superintendent of the State, possesses a few pronounced urban characteristics and amenities. Although leaving room for vagueness and discretion, the last criterion was intended to cover newly founded industrial areas, large housing settlements, or places of tourist importance which have been recently served with all civic amenities (*Census of India, 1961*, 1964a: 51).

In an interesting study on urbanity based on the first three census criteria (the fourth was omitted for being somewhat "vague and arbitrary"), Bose (1968) found that only sixty percent of urban places as defined in the 1961 census satisfied all of the first three requirements; and if the municipal status criterion were added to the above three, the percentage of qualifying places would drop to forty-three percent. He suggested this to be indicative of an overestimation of the urban population in the census. This finding further reiterates the need for a clarification of the urban concept.

Currently, in the study of urbanization, behavioral, structural and demographic approaches are applied to a wide range of analytical problems; but each of these approaches faces the usual difficulties of definition and measurement (Lampard, 1965: 519-520). The behavioral approach focuses on the behavior pattern of the individuals; the structural approach concentrates on the general behavior pattern of whole populations and "gives primary recognition to the differential ordering of occupations or industries within a given territorial space." In the demographic approach, on the other hand, emphasis is placed on the population-concentration process in space (Lampard, 1965: 519-520). In defining the urban concept or, to be more exact, in defining the urban area, the Indian census has relied mostly on the structural and demographic variables. Behavioral aspects—such as social values, caste, and kinship—are not taken into consideration, perhaps because there is a great deal of similarity in such institutions between urban and rural areas in India, as suggested by the fragmented studies on such phenomena (Glass, 1964: 25; UNESCO, 1964: 41). Consequently, it is not clear to what extent designated areas with political-administrative boundaries portray urban characteristics; whether the urban characteristics originate and emanate from a central core in the urban place; and whether they show any decline outward from the core and cease altogether after the arbitrary urban boundary line is crossed.

Inquiries of this nature have led to a good deal of discussion on such topics as rural-urban "dichotomy" and "continuum." Simply put, the dichotomy hypothesis assumes a distinctive differentiation of urban places from rural places, and the term "continuum" refers to an environment "neither completely rural nor completely urban but rather as occupying a position somewhere between the two extremes" (Gibbs, 1961: 467).[3] While it is not the purpose here to discuss these concepts in detail, it may be noted that in the above light the Indian census definition of urban places, since it is based on a set of urban-qualifying criteria, appears to be dichotomous in nature. However, research on these concepts shows a growing concern among social scientists over rural-urban differentiation. Some have coined new terminologies, such as "rurban villages" or "semi-urban pockets," and have drawn attention to them as distinctly separate categories with unique characteristics.[4] In a thoughtful paper, Mukherjee (1963) analysed the controversy from a sociological perspective; he concluded that the concepts of dichotomy and continuum in the context of urbanization and consequent social development may be of limited value in India since a significant rural-urban difference is not evident, and that, therefore, a cause-and-effect relationship between an urban pattern of living and social change cannot be established.

Furthermore, Yadava (1970: 301) has stated that:

> People may become urbanized in their thinking and behavior although they may not move to a town or city. They may not move from agricultural work to industrial work and still they may be urbanized. The contention here is that though urbanism (urban way of life) is distinct from peasant way of life, they need not be exclusive of each other.... Rural-urban dichotomy is a useful conceptual frame of reference only and is not a reality.

It is true that in terms of some structural and demographic elements, an urban way of life and the rural-urban difference can readily be recognized. Among various distinguishing features the proportion of migrants, frequency of change of residence, ownership of houses, and occupational structure might be considered important. However, unlike the large urban centers, small towns might have many features (caste or religion-based residence, household or tenure pattern, and so on) common with the villages (UNESCO, 1964: 43). Considering the above, it would be difficult to draw any definitive conclusion on the question of the existence of a rural-urban dichotomy or continuum without a thorough investigation based on "the formal quantitative record and ... the help of more complex, more intensive, longitudinal studies" (Glass, 1964: 26).

The preceding discussion points indirectly toward a less controversial but equally pertinent matter: the existence of similarities or differences among the urban places in India. No matter what approach is adopted for defining the urban place, homogeneity in urban features would be an exception rather than a rule among various urban places within a nation. Degree of "urbanness" may vary with size, function, location, and various other factors; and therefore it is apparent that research should not only be focused on the concepts of urbanity and rurality, but also on the magnitude of variation of urban phenomena in diverse contexts. Theoretically speaking, in terms of urban attributes, there should be a continuum among different-sized urban places, as observed by Davis (1951: 134-144) and others. However, a study based on census data has revealed that in contrast to western countries there is a lack of continuity in urban structural pattern by size in Indian urban places of over 50,000 population. Due to a lack of adequate organization within the diverse productive enterprises and insufficient politicosocial cohesion, Indian cities tend to remain "segmented" (Namboodiri, 1966: 34).

While a formal operational definition of "urban" is useful, it should be kept in mind that processes leading to urbanization are complex and any analysis of the phenomena would require clear perception of the interplay of many forces. Thus, while an increase of population in cities and towns might not be too surprising (see Figure 1), the underlying forces that lead to the movement of people and their clustering in and around particular places would certainly warrant some understanding. The process of urbanization in India, as in any other country, is a reflection of the existing socioeconomic conditions and major institutional changes in the society. For example, a deliberate policy of limiting the size and function of certain urban places may affect the urban structural pattern and, in turn, a change in the "scale of urbanization" may become apparent.[5] Such a policy might promote the growth of a particular group of cities or towns for sound economic reasons; however, it may also create some sociopolitical and spatial problems. During the last decades of economic planning, a great many institutional changes have been induced, and their potential impact on the urban scene in India has to be borne in mind. Along with changes in the societal parameters, the urban concept changes over time. If these changing aspects are given due consideration, an assessment of the patterns and problems of urbanization would be more meaningful.

The Indian census, as noted earlier, delineated urban places on the basis of certain criteria which do not take into consideration the individual and/or collective space-related behavior patterns which may be termed as "urban values." It has been argued that the study of urbanization, particularly from perspectives of social change, should stress human variables as, in Lampard's words, "the fundamental distribution of population is . . . ecological, and not economic" (1965: 549). Although the space-related activity may be economic in nature, it subsumes an expression of behavior patterns of individuals or groups. Thus, in conformity to the urban characteristics in some other developing nations, many Indian cities portray an "incompletely-urban" outlook or "appear hybrids rather than full-fledged urbanized units" (Chatterjee, 1968: 198). The rural elements that so commonly appear in Indian urban settings—for example, wandering cattle, the presence of bullock carts, or vendors selling cowdung-cakes on the main streets—reflect certain aspects of socioeconomic conditions of the urban dwellers normally not considered in defining an urban environment. Without particular reference to the

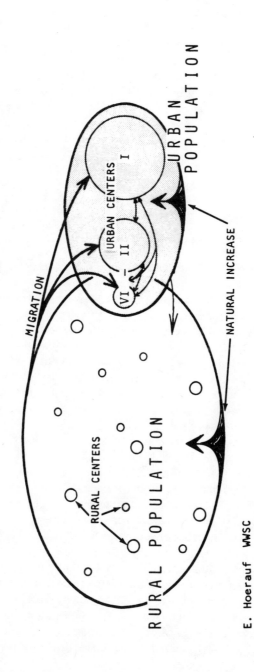

Figure 1: URBANIZATION PROCESS (HYPOTHETICAL)

prevalent social institutions—such as the gift of cattle at the *Sradha* ceremonies—it would be rather difficult to explain the presence of wandering cattle in large metropolises of India and the habit of throwing fruit and vegetable peelings into the streets.[6] Therefore, it is imperative for an understanding of the urban environment in its entirety—its uniqueness due to the presence of certain features, or absence of some common characteristics of Western urbanization—that proper consideration be given to the role of "urban values" as these affect the structural and demographic features of urbanization. As Anderson (1959: 7) observed:

> Without discounting in the least the statistics on population and occupations, we must also recognize that before referring to a person or an aggregate of people as urban or not urban we must take account of their thinking and behavior, which may be very urban, very rural, or some urban-rural mixture.

In light of the above, the term "urban" may be said to be incompletely defined; and although the Indian census provides a set of urban-qualifying criteria, due to the varying emphasis given to the interpretation of these criteria by the states, it is difficult to ensure strict comparability of urban characteristics on a regional basis. However, the present census offers many features that are useful for research in the urban field. Although some of the fundamental questions such as "what is urban?" or "what is rural?" and issues on "rural-urban dichotomy" or "continuum" are yet to be solved, the census certainly has created a fertile ground in its ample statistical load for discussion of such issues with a greater degree of sophistication than hitherto.

The census categorization of urban places into six classes by size is useful for an understanding of urbanization in spatial and temporal contexts.[7] Since, as a result of regional development efforts and industrial decentralization, greater research emphasis is being placed on the study of smaller centers, census grouping of places on the basis of size facilitates research in the above area. Availability of data on urban places by size groups has also enabled researchers to study the urban continuum concept in order to identify any "continuous gradations" and "consistent variations" that would shed light on patterns of urban environment.

Data on selected structural and demographic factors in the census reveal the regional variation in the urbanization process that might have implication for planning, and also for reorientation, or modification of existing programs. Even while noting the limitations inherent in the census concept of urban (because the behavioral and value factors were not taken into account), it must be admitted that for researchers with an objective of examining the ecological and economic aspects of "urban dynamics" (Hanna and Hanna, 1971: 8), the structural and demographic data provided in the *Census of India* are invaluable.

URBAN INDUSTRIAL LINKAGES

The interacting and interrelated nature of urban and industrial development has been the subject of much thought and discussion ever since the impact of industrialization in the West has become apparent. It is true, as some scholars have pointed out, that these two, though interrelated,[8] are not necessarily identical, as one without the other has been experienced (see, for example Harris, 1962: 263; Heberle, 1948: 29; Wirth, 1957: 50). Questions have been raised such as "whether there exists a necessary strict correlation between the two processes, whether industrial growth cannot take place by a process of planned decentralization, and whether, on the other hand, urbanization can appear without concomitant industrialization" (Hoselitz, 1957: 42).

Though the questions are still, to a major extent, unanswered, it is accepted that industrialization plays an important part in the growth of urbanization. The multiplier and cumulative effects of urban-industrial development have been apparent in many nations that have been touched by these phenomena ever since the Industrial Revolution. In a developing country like India, industrialization has been termed "the most important factor influencing the growth of urbanization, urban centers, and general economic development" (Basu, 1965: 24). Although this view may need to be modified, the important role of industrial undertakings in promoting the growth of certain points or regions in India, and for that matter in any developing economy, can hardly be overemphasized. The experience of some often rapidly developing Asian countries, such as Japan or Taiwan, show that these countries have achieved higher economic development by expanding their industrial production and modernizing agricultural sector of the economy along with the development of transport and communication in contrast to such countries as India or Pakistan where "low urban ratio" is associated with "low rates of economic development" (Ham 1973: 108).

This does not obscure the fact that long before the advent of industrialization, the world knew urban centers of splendor and distinction. However, "preindustrial cities have always functioned primarily as governmental and religious centers, and only secondarily as commercial establishments" (Sjoberg, 1965: 216). This was true particularly in Asia (e.g., India and China) even though "many of them were also the centers of extensive trade and bases for highly developed artisan production" (Murphy, 1972: 252). In India, along with the cities of administrative or religious origin, there were handicraft and trade centers with an "extensive export trade to the Middle East and to Southeast Asia" which, with the beginnings of European control over India, gradually lost ground and decayed; and "by the mid-nineteenth century the new urbanism, based on European incentive, had begun" (Crane, 1955: 470). In the words of Murphy (1972: 254): "They [the traditional Asian cities] were outposts of the West, . . . where the commercial and industrial revolutions had been planted for foreign profit and where the seeds of Asia's modern transformation also germinated."

Commerce, even in the halcyon days of the precolonial India, was of necessity limited by the locational advantages that certain centers offered, and did not contribute to urbanization on a large scale. Its nature changed in the decades that followed the landing of the first European on the Indian subcontinent. With the advent of industrialization—with its burgeoning service industry and a greater emphasis on improved transport, storage, and communication facilities—the impact of commerce on urbanization expanded on the one hand; while on the other, it became only a facet of the total array of forces that make up the commercialization process of present-day societies. As Murphy (1972: 255, 256) has described this process in the context of India and China:

> Western type commercial industrial centers have drawn labor, trade goods for processing or export, and raw materials from countryside, and at the same time have extended the domestic market for urban-produced goods through a growing transport network, stimulating the increasing commercialization of the economy as a whole. . . .
>
> Million class cities have become numerous in both countries, topping a new urban hierarchy which includes a major and rapidly growing commercial center served by railways in every state or province, many with several such centers. Spurred originally by colonial investments in trade and manufacturing, they have grown predominantly on the basis of rural inmigration from the increasingly overpopulated countryside.

The supposition of an ideal balance or equilibrium between urbanization and industrialization or economic development has led some scholars to the much discussed and controversial concept of over-urbanization (which has propagated various other terms such as hyper-urbanism, and so on). Hauser (1957: 9), one of the proponents of this theory, argues that, "It is true to say that Asia is over-urbanized in relation to its degree of economic development. At comparable levels of urbanization, the developed countries of today had a correspondingly greater proportion of their labor force engaged in non-agricultural occupations" (see also Hoselitz, 1957: 44-46).

Among many other contributing factors, this condition is thought to be caused basically by an excessive rural-urban migration; and it is felt that "rural push," because of "the inability of a limited agricultural area to support the rapidly rising number of young people" (Hoselitz, 1957: 45), rather than urban attractions and amenities or "pull," is mostly responsible for this cityward movement. "One consequence of this premature migration is the high rate of unemployment and/or marginal employment in the great cities of Asia and Africa" (Abu-Lughad, 1965: 313). Other consequences are the lack of adequate facilities in housing, transportation, recreation, and all other urban amenities. Sovani (1966: 1-13) is one of a number of scholars (Abu-Lughad, 1965; Browning, 1967: 73-74; Harris, 1959: 196; Kamerschen, 1969) to critically examine this concept of over-urbanization on several pertinent grounds. Neither a discussion of the nature of these arguments and counter-arguments nor a debate as to whether India is over-urbanized or not, would be within the scope of the present work. However, even without going through the technicalities of the term and the precise nature and validity of the "push" or "pull" factors, it can be said that some of the consequences of this so-called over-urbanization—in the form of a "disproportion between the costs of urban growth and the maintenance of proper facilities for urban dwellers and the earning capacity of the people congregated in cities" (Hoselitz, 1957: 44), urban unemployment, and underemployment—are very much apparent in the urban scene of India today, particularly in the larger urban centers.

As to the relationship between the process of urbanization and industrialization in India during 1951-1961, observations and comments of a wide range and scope abound in the literature. Bose (1961: 256) has noted:

In the last few years both expert and laymen have talked of "over-urbanization" in India, a term indicative of a rate of urban growth which is not warranted by the prevailing level of industrialization and economic development. But the Census figures seem to indicate that during the last decade rapid industrialization has been accompanied by slow urbanization. Does this mean that there is now under-urbanization of India?

Peach, on the other hand, has maintained that "the match-makers of policy [in India] have aimed at industrialization without urbanization and achieved urbanization without industrialization" (1968: 297); and further that "the policies of industrialization with urbanization have become a reality of urbanization without industry" (1968: 303). Comments like these provide the impetus for examination of the current urban-industrial situation in India.

Change in occupational structure has long been considered one of the most pertinent indices to measure the extent and nature of industrialization and urbanization. The widely accepted but recently much-debated Clark-Fisher hypothesis, for example, maintains that with the development of an economy from a primitive-agricultural to an urban-industrial stage, there is a gradual shift in its occupational structure from primary to secondary to tertiary sectors, with a positive correlation between employment in the tertiary sector and per capita real income. This thesis has found two of its most severe critics in Bauer and Yami (1951), who have challenged it on both analytical and statistical grounds, and a series of highly interesting arguments and counter-arguments has followed since then (see, for example, Bauer and Yami, 1954; Fisher, 1952; Mehta, 1961: 177-179; Rottenberg, 1953). Hauser (1957: 6-7), while maintaining that "economic development . . . results almost invariably in an accentuation of the process of urbanization . . . [and] implies a change in the occupational structure of the working force towards non-agricultural activities," echoed the thoughts of many when he said that

> the preponderence of tertiary industries in urban areas of several countries of Asia does not represent the evolution of these economies from a secondary to a tertiary basis—movement identified as progressive in the long run—but signifies the growth of marginal employment and low productive service industries, especially retail trading and domestic services.

This view is supported by other scholars,[9] and in general the secondary sector is considered to be more of an indicator of economic (and urban) development in India than the tertiary sector.[10] More empirical studies are needed before any satisfactory conclusion can be reached on this issue.[11] However, in viewing the urban-industrial picture, or in assessing trends in the sectoral shifts in India, these factors should be taken into consideration in order to ensure against any hasty generalization.

THE URBAN–INDUSTRIAL PATTERN

In view of the very high urban population increase in India both in terms of absolute numbers and rate of growth during the 1940s, several estimates were made indicating an even higher and more spectacular growth of urban population in the fifties. The census figures of 1961 did not quite meet such expectations. While the variation of urban population during 1951-1961 was about 26%, the proportionate growth was much less, being only 3.80% (1951-1961) as compared to 24.66% in the 1941-1951 period. This situation has led many to believe that the "tempo" of urbanization has slowed down somewhat and has aroused interest among many researchers to investigate the apparent reasons for such change. The spatial pattern of urbanization in 1961 and urban growth during 1951-1961 are shown in Figures 2 and 3, respectively.

However, in the study of urbanization in India, particular attention must be given to the changed 1961 census definition of "urban" when analysing the growth between 1951-1961. Some consider this retardation in the urban growth "more apparent than real" because of the definitional change (Nath, 1966: 120-121). Bose estimated the decade's growth of population at about 38%, somewhat comparable to the increase in the earlier decade (cited in Nath, 1966: 121). Even the census has taken note of the fact that, because of change in urban definition, a number of towns under the 1951 census were eliminated from the urban category in the census of 1961, and that "if the 1951 Census towns had all been retained the resultant population would just have fitted the historic trend of urban growth between 1901-1951 . . . [even though] it would still have belied widely-held expectations of rapid increase" (*Census of India, 1961*, 1962: LX). It seems then that, but for the high expectations and the change in definition, urban growth in India in the decade of 1951-1961 would probably not have appeared as stunted as it does now when the census figures under the new definition of urban are compared with the predicted figures. However, even conceding the role of the above factors in portraying a less than accurate growth pattern, the somewhat sluggish nature of urbanization during the decade can hardly be denied.

The reasons for this apparent slower growth rate in urban population are complex and varied. Among several possible explanations offered by individual scholars, the major ones seem to be: (1) the absence of heavy migration due to war and partition of the subcontinent, as in the previous decade; (2) failure of the local urban bodies to attract migrants through investment programs or other lucrative offers; (3) decline in urban sex ratio due to lack of adequate housing and other urban amenities; and (4)

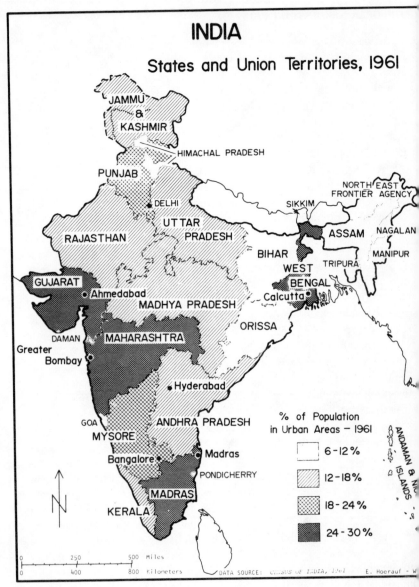

INDIA

States and Union Territories, 1961

JAMMU & KASHMIR

HIMACHAL PRADESH

PUNJAB

DELHI

NORTH EAST FRONTIER AGENCY

SIKKIM

RAJASTHAN

UTTAR PRADESH

ASSAM

NAGALAN

BIHAR

MANIPUR

WEST BENGAL

TRIPURA

GUJARAT

Ahmedabad

Calcutta

MADHYA PRADESH

DAMAN

ORISSA

MAHARASHTRA

Greater Bombay

Hyderabad

GOA

ANDHRA PRADESH

ANDAMAN & NIC. ISLANDS

MYSORE

Bangalore

Madras

PONDICHERRY

MADRAS

KERALA

% of Population in Urban Areas – 1961

- 6 – 12 %
- 12 – 18 %
- 18 – 24 %
- 24 – 30 %

| 0 | 250 | 500 | Miles |
| 0 | 400 | 800 | Kilometers |

DATA SOURCE: CENSUS OF INDIA, 1961   E. Hoerauf – W

Figure 2.

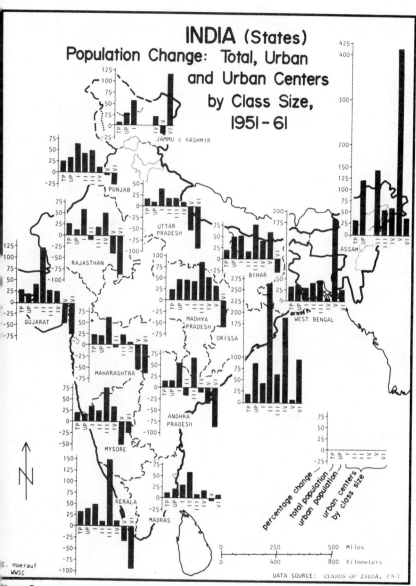

INDIA (States)
Population Change: Total, Urban and Urban Centers by Class Size, 1951-61

DATA SOURCE: *CENSUS OF INDIA, 1961*

E. Hoerauf
WWSC

Figure 3.

99401

increased opportunities for the rural population by creation of various rural development programs (*Census of India 1961*, 1962: LX; Bose, 1961: 272).

Although the rate of urbanization may be considered rather slow over the decade, the volume and rate of concentration of the urban population in larger urban places in 1961 has been remarkable. As Table 1 indicates, nearly 45% of the total urban population of India resided in the Class I centers in 1961. With a growth rate of about 48%, these cities added over eleven million people to their population during the 1951-1961 decade. [12]

As mentioned earlier, one of the indicators of general economic development through the industrialization-urbanization process is considered to be a shift in the occupational pattern of the labor force. The proponents of this theory assume a shift in the employed labor force from primary to secondary and tertiary sectors, as the economy changes from a pre-industrial to an industrial stage. A cursory look at the Indian male labor force data in Table 2 over the past decade reveals that, during that period, there has not been any appreciable change in the occupational structure of the economy.

Among the states and union territories for which data were available, with the exception of Gujarat, Rajasthan, and West Bengal, the proportion of male workers in the primary sector either declined or remained more or less stable over the decade; whereas, except for Gujarat, Kerala, and Manipur, the number of workers increased in the secondary sector. In the tertiary sector, while nearly 60% of the states failed to record an increase, Kerala and Manipur showed more than a 5% increase in workers. The all-India pattern revealed an increase of 1.65% in the proportion of workers in secondary activities; the primary sector declined by almost the same amount, as the tertiary sector recorded a negligible increase of .01%.[13]

TABLE 1

POPULATION CHANGE IN CITIES AND TOWNS: 1951-1961

Size Class	1961 Urban Population (%)	1951-1961	
		Change in Number	% Change
I: 100,000 & over	44.50	+11,394,182	48.02
II: 50,000-99,999	12.17	+ 1,905,145	24.99
III: 20,000-49,999	19.95	+ 4,634,473	41.70
IV: 10,000-19,999	14.32	+ 1,920,974	20.48
V: 5,000-9,999	8.04	− 2,166,607	−25.46
VI: under 5,000	1.13	− 1,195,498	−57.33

SOURCE: Census of India, 1961 (1964: 272).

TABLE 2

PERCENTAGE DISTRIBUTION OF MALE WORKERS BY THREE SECTORS IN STATES AND SELECTED UNION TERRITORIES: 1951-1961

	Total Male Workers (I–IX)	Primary (I, II, III) 1951	1961	Change 51-61	Secondary (IV, V, VI) 1951	1961	Change 51-61	Tertiary (VII, VIII, IX) 1951	1961	Change 51-61
Andhra Pradesh	100	68.37	67.03	— 1.34	13.03	15.14	2.11	18.60	17.83	— .77
Assam	100	81.37	77.09	— 4.28	3.55	4.62	1.07	15.08	18.29	3.21
Bihar	100	85.00	77.51	— 7.49	3.89	8.39	4.50	11.11	14.10	2.99
Gujarat	100	60.40	65.00	4.60	14.50	14.00	— .50	20.00	17.00	— 3.00
Kerala	100	55.76	46.12	— 9.64	17.52	16.45	— 1.07	26.72	37.43	10.71
Madhya Pradesh	100	78.57	77.29	— 1.28	8.83	9.75	.92	12.60	12.96	.36
Madras	100	61.85	59.44	— 2.41	15.35	15.91	.56	22.80	24.65	1.85
Maharashtra	100	62.00	62.40	.40	15.20	16.10	.90	20.10	19.70	— .40
Mysore	100	69.50	69.42	— .08	12.64	13.71	1.07	17.86	16.87	— .99
Orissa	100	76.93	76.69	.26	6.94	7.28	.34	16.63	16.03	— .60
Punjab	100	65.12	61.29	— 3.83	9.32	15.52	6.20	25.56	23.19	— 2.37
Rajasthan	100	72.14	74.22	2.08	9.80	10.51	.71	18.04	15.27	— 2.77
Uttar Pradesh	100	74.21	73.34	.87	9.00	10.23	1.23	16.79	16.43	— .36
West Bengal	100	55.46	57.54	2.08	16.19	16.84	.65	28.35	25.62	— 2.73
Andaman & Nicobar Islands	100	57.06	47.10	— 9.96	11.13	32.34	21.21	31.81	20.56	—11.25
Delhi	100	8.23	6.00	— 2.23	25.11	26.88	1.77	66.66	67.12	.46
Himachal Pradesh	100	90.11	78.94	—11.17	4.12	10.60	6.48	5.77	10.46	4.69
Manipur	100	81.56	78.06	— 3.50	7.42	5.53	— 1.89	11.02	16.41	5.39
Tripura	100	74.85	73.40	— 1.45	4.12	6.23	2.11	21.03	20.37	— .66
All India	100	69.64	67.98	— 1.66	11.03	12.68	1.65	19.33	19.34	.01

SOURCES: Census of India, 1961 (1962: 406-407, 412-413);
Census of India, 1961 (1968: 28-29, 30-31).

However, as far as the sheer volume of population is concerned, it is rather impressive to note that during 1951-1961 in the urban areas alone, there have been increases of over 2.1 million and 2.3 million male workers in the secondary and tertiary sectors, respectively (Bose, 1965: 7). The spatial distribution of change in urban population and in male labor force in the nonagricultural sectors of the states is presented in Figure 4.

The interrelationship between urban and industrial development patterns by states can be observed in Table 3. The coefficients of urbanization and industrialization (with figures over 1.00 denoting a higher than average concentration) reflect that, with the exception of Kerala,[14] the highly urbanized states are also the ones with above average concentration of manufacturing industry. It may be noted that, again excepting Kerala, the six states with the highest coefficients of urbanization and industrialization also rank highest in the scale of urbanization. In view of the fact that "in general, the greater the concentration of the urban and the total population in a large size class, the greater the scale of urbanization" (Gibbs, 1966: 171), this association seems to point toward an affinity of industries with larger urban centers.

TABLE 3

COEFFICIENT OF URBANIZATION AND INDUSTRIALIZATION, AND SCALE OF URBANIZATION OF THE STATES: 1961

	Coefficient of Urbanization[a]	Coefficient of Industrialization[b]	Scale of Urbanization[c]
Andhra Pradesh	0.97	0.60	0.66
Assam	0.43	0.48	0.22
Bihar	0.47	0.52	0.30
Gujarat	1.43	1.50	1.00
Jammu & Kashmir	0.93	0.52	0.58
Kerala	0.84	2.23	0.57
Madhya Pradesh	0.79	0.47	0.48
Madras	1.49	1.31	0.99
Maharashtra	1.57	1.63	1.24
Mysore	1.24	0.93	0.80
Orissa	0.35	0.27	0.20
Punjab	1.12	1.18	0.70
Rajasthan	0.91	0.42	0.57
Uttar Pradesh	0.72	0.66	0.53
West Bengal	1.36	2.69	1.10

a. The ratio of urban to total population of state divided by the ratio of urban total population for All-India; see Basu (1965: 25).

b. The ratio of employment in manufacturing industry to total workers of state divided by the ratio of manufacturing to total workers in India (Basu, 1965: 25).

c. Based on a formula devised by Gibbs (1966: 171): $Su = \sum xy$, where Su is the measure, x is the proportion of urban population in each class size and over, and y the proportion of the total population in the same units (class size and over).

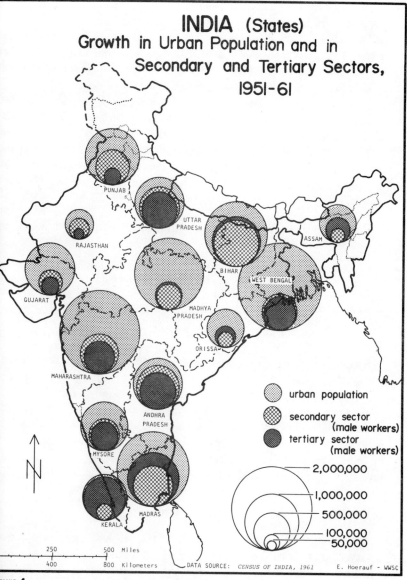

INDIA (States)
Growth in Urban Population and in
Secondary and Tertiary Sectors,
1951-61

PUNJAB

UTTAR
PRADESH

RAJASTHAN

ASSAM

BIHAR

GUJARAT

WEST BENGAL

MADHYA
PRADESH

ORISSA

MAHARASHTRA

ANDHRA
PRADESH

MYSORE

MADRAS

KERALA

urban population

secondary sector
(male workers)

tertiary sector
(male workers)

2,000,000

1,000,000

500,000

100,000
50,000

250   500 Miles

400   800 Kilometers

DATA SOURCE: *CENSUS OF INDIA, 1961*   E. Hoerauf - WWSC

Figure 4.

In terms of the concentration of industrial establishments in urban areas, it is notable that—as in many well-developed countries—a highly disproportionate share of industrial undertakings are located in the relatively larger urban centers of India. As Nath has observed, only about 35% of the total undertakings in the private sector are concentrated in urban places with populations below 100,000. Interestingly, the share of these larger cities in the fastest growing sectors of industry—namely, metals and metal products, machinery and equipment, and chemical and allied products—is around 75% (Nath, 1966: 129).

The much-discussed reasons and theories for this concentration lead to the simple conclusion that at the present time in India the investor finds the most ideal environment for his enterprise to be the larger urban centers:

> For entrepreneurship, in the best of circumstances, involves assumption of risk for the long-run chance of profit. In the early stages of the nation's industrial growth, with undeveloped markets, untrained labor, little in the way of infrastructure or communications to outlying regions, the factor of risk is minimized by maximum accessibility to opportunities for markets, labor, transports, and utilities. In underdeveloped nations, location in the largest cities provides the best physical setting for effective industrialization and economic growth [Rivkin, 1967: 124].

Some of the larger cities, like Calcutta, Bombay, and Madras, developed the necessary infrastructure from the very beginning of the colonial era. By virtue of their location and certain administrative functions, the "milionaire" cities in India took a lead in the national development process, and provided enough incentive to attract a wide variety of industries. Therefore, in the process of urbanization, the larger urban units in India have assumed a special role, and a close association between urbanization and industrialization is likely to be evident in such cities.

DECENTRALIZATION: SOME CONSIDERATIONS

Throughout the history of urbanization, it has commonly been observed that, after an optimum level is reached, concentration of industries and population in the larger urban areas creates a wide range of problems gradually reducing the advantages which had attracted the industrial units and the people initially.[15] For example, land values in cities tend to increase at a rate fast enough to pose a serious problem. Along with this, the overhead costs of industries go up with the cost of transport, storage, maintenance, and production of their goods and services. A deterioration in the living and working conditions of the laborers (as a possible result of the falling man-land ratio) may manifest itself in the form of labor discontent and a below-optimum efficiency level. Slums; overcrowding; lack of adequate transport, recreational, and sanitary facilities; housing shortages; and congestion are some of the all too apparent and common drawbacks of concentration that urban dwellers face in the largest cities. However, the irony of urban-industrial growth is, that—even with all these disadvantages, drawbacks, and discomforts—once the momentum is started, the process of further concentration goes on until and unless some well planned effort from within or without is exerted to control and redirect this concentration.[16]

To deal with various urban environmental problems on the one hand and an acceleration of regional disparities on the other, resulting from a progressive concentration of industries and population in certain large urban centers, several measures have been suggested by planners, economists, geographers and others, both in India and abroad. Of these, decentralization and "selective concentration" of existing or new industries emerge as the key factors essential in any attempt to alleviate these problems. Relocating existing industries away from the large centers, attracting new industries and migrants to the smaller places, encouraging emigration from the overcongested large urban centers, and creating new industrial towns[17] are considered to be some of the ways to achieve this end.

In spite of the inherent conceptual and definitional differences as to the nature, scope, and size of the urban centers, the overall focus of planning seems to be on the urban units of submetropolitan sizes. It is believed that developing these centers would tend to even out the imbalances of lopsided urban industrial growth in certain areas of India. With respect to relocation or creation of industries, it is suggested that a balance has to be achieved between such objectives as reduction of regional disparities and improving the backward areas, and the economic considerations of overhead costs, growth potential, resource and labor availability, and expected returns. Any indiscriminate planning policy with only maximization of the profits or returns in mind and without due consideration for regional development is undesirable. At the same time if adequate consideration for the economics of location for industrial establishments is not given, there will be wastage or draining of resources. As Jakobson and Prakash (1971: 35) have suggested:

> The application of such concepts as new towns, growth poles, counter magnets, and dispensed centralization, as suggested by the United Nations' Urbanization Seminar, seem to us valid concepts

only if the social and economic costs of their implementation are justifiable in relation to the resources at hand. Regardless of their appeal, a premature new towns policy, for example, leads only to excessive costs and a waste of scarce capital and energy—not to mention their total impact on the process of urbanization. This example is clearly demonstrated in the case of new towns in India.[Italics added].

As to the specific size of urban centers most suitable for industrialization, it is generally believed that the medium-sized towns have better prospects than the small semi-urban centers or the large overcongested metropolitan cities. The existence of the basic urban amenities, a necessary infrastructure, along with other administrative and institutional facilities make such units more attractive to the prospective entrepreneurs and also to potential migrants, than the urban size classes in either extreme.[18]

Some smaller urban centers in rural settings, however, if endowed with sufficient resources, may be suitable for some particular resource-oriented industries and may well be the beginning of a new growth point (Mathai, 1965 and Thacker, 1965: 39). Cities with relatively lower levels of industrial congestion may also be considered for industrial relocation.[19] Indian scholars, administrators, and planners have suggested that the government help in creating the basic facilities, such as acquisition of land, power, water supply, transport system, housing, and so on, needed for industries and the industrial population, with the hope that such development would attract prospective entrepreneurs and migrants to these locations.[20] Parenthetically, it may be noted, that by virtue of their location in a rural setting, these "semi-urban pockets" or "rurban centers" would have the added potential advantage of stimulating a rural-urban physical and cultural interaction and diffusion of ideas, thus creating an environment for "social industrialization" (Basu, 1965: 29) which may be sought to ease the so-called "rural-urban dichotomy."

Among other measures, it is anticipated that the establishment of satellite towns around large cities would not only ease the existing urban problems in such cities, as the experience of various western countries has shown, it would also encourage emigration from the mother cities. Such satellite towns, as suggested, may be of 50,000 to 80,000 population at a distance of 30 to 50 kilometers from the city (Khurana, 1965: 21). If developed around the larger cities of India with careful planning, they could be expected to modify the spatial pattern of urbanization and heavy concentration of industries in the existing larger urban centers. Depending on the specific locational advantages and the nature of industries to be developed or relocated to such towns, there is no doubt that some of the benefits of the urban-industrial environment already existing at the large centers could at least be partially shared by the satellite towns.

PLANNING, POLICY AND PRACTICE

In analysing the plans and achievements in India, the overwhelmingly complex and difficult nature of planning in an economy like India's should be kept in mind. Any analysis or criticism done in retrospect has the advantage of viewing the plans and their consequences from the perspectives of time and space; while the planners, no matter how equipped they are with past history and future projections, are still very much restricted by their time, their vision obstructed by their particular period.

Among the diverse and often conflicting opinions on the plans, policies, and achievements in the context of India's urban-industrial development, one of the more consistent criticisms against the first three five-year plans in general, and the first plan in particular, is that spatial factors were not taken under adequate consideration in planning (Desai, 1968: 450; Natarajan, 1968; Vagale, 1965). Optimal allocation of resources on a sectoral basis for maximization of returns with an inherent reliance on the "spread effect" or the "trickle-down mechanism," rather than regional development in a spatial context and a balanced urbanization, was the dominant motive behind the earlier plans, particularly the first five-year plan (Natarajan, 1968: 25-26).[21] However, this trickle-down mechanism did not work well in India (see Berry and Rao, 1968: 25-27); and with time, the planners became progressively aware of the regional disparities and urban-industrial imbalances due to excessive concentration of industries in certain growth points. Thus, urban-industrial policies with a spatial dimension emerged. At the beginning of the second plan period, the second Industrial Policy Resolution of 1956, for example, aimed to reduce regional disparities in the level of development:

The idea of balanced coordinated development of industrial and agricultural sectors on a regional basis was emphasized. It also underlined the need of providing basic facilities of power, water supply, transport and communications to depressed areas with industrial potential [Raj, 1969: 302].

In view of this goal, the second and third plans emphasized village and small-scale industries in building up a stable and decentralized industrial sector and in alleviating the regional disparities by creating employment opportunities in the backward or underdeveloped regions.[22] The

Industrial Estates Programme, which was first envisaged during the later years of the first plan, was strengthened during the subsequent plans with special emphasis on locational policies, "as a tool to raise the living standards of the masses by showing the benefits of industrialization over wider areas, approaching a more balanced development of ragions and by tapping unused resources of small capital and manpower" (Raj, 1965: 68).

However, even though the program has met success in some regions it failed to meet the overall objectives in others.[23] Some social scientists have pointed out that India "committed two mistakes that must be avoided in developing rural industries—putting city factories in rural areas and failing to integrate rural industries with agriculture" (Owens and Shaw, 1972: 114). Elaborating further on the first factor, for example, they wrote that

> many of the factories set up in the estates represented the *relocation* of city-oriented factories rather than the kind of factories needed to integrate a local urban center with its rural hinterland. Factories in these estates were producing or assembling such things as radios, circuit breakers, gears and gear boxes, nitric acid, and steel furniture. Most of these products can be manufactured more cheaply in the major engineering centers of Bombay, Calcutta, Madras and Delhi. In addition, transportation costs were inflated because many of the raw materials were shipped from the big cities to the rural town for production, and then shipped back to the big cities because the market for these products is in cities, not small towns and villages. Because these are the wrong factories in wrong place production costs are inflated [Owens and Shaw, 1972: 114-115; italics added].

Also, as Figure 5 indicates, contrary to public and governmental expectations and to the basic principles of the Industrial Estates policy, almost two-thirds of the total employment in the industrial estates was concentrated in urban places of over 100,000 population (Nath, 1966: 129; see also Roth, 1970: 394-395).

The effort on the part of the government to decentralize industries on a regional basis and away from big cities has been relatively more successful in the public sector. Of the industries licensed during the first three five-year plans, about 70% have been set up in "small towns" and "greenfield locations." However, so far as the private sector is concerned, the major urban centers with their already existing necessary infrastructure and external economies are still the main attractions for industries. Between 1952 and 1964, over 60% of new industrial units have been located in such cities (Nath, 1966: 129-130).

This has led some to suggest that since the Licensing Committee set up

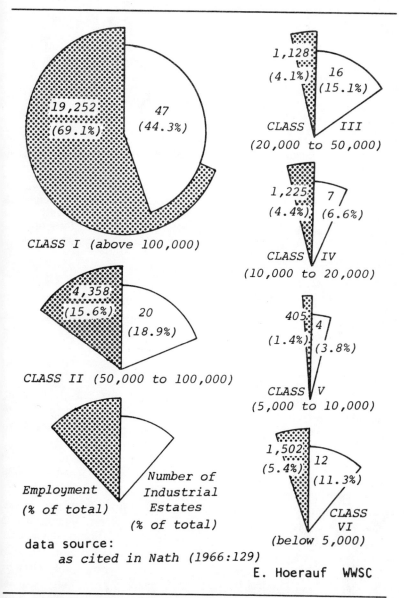

CLASS I (above 100,000)

19,252 (69.1%)   47 (44.3%)

CLASS III (20,000 to 50,000)

1,128 (4.1%)   16 (15.1%)

CLASS IV (10,000 to 20,000)

1,225 (4.4%)   7 (6.6%)

CLASS II (50,000 to 100,000)

4,358 (15.6%)   20 (18.9%)

CLASS V (5,000 to 10,000)

405 (1.4%)   4 (3.8%)

Employment (% of total)

Number of Industrial Estates (% of total)

CLASS VI (below 5,000)

1,502 (5.4%)   12 (11.3%)

data source:
    as cited in Nath (1966:129)

E. Hoerauf   WWSC

Figure 5: INDUSTRIAL ESTATES BY URBAN CLASS SIZE (1963)

under the Industries (Development and Regulation) Act of 1951 has the power to grant permission on condition of "location of the undertaking,"

> the Committee could thus exercise its powers to ensure a suitable pattern of industrial dispersion. But the Committee did not apply any clear-cut criteria for decision-making on the location of industries to be licensed. They did not pay much attention to this aspect and were mainly occupied with questions of the types and scales of industries, their potentialities, regulation, and control [Raj, 1969: 302].[24]

The desirability and practicality of such a control, however, has been questioned:

> While admittedly useful, it is doubtful whether such a policy can be formulated, much less enforced. The states would certainly be reluctant to impose such a self-denying ordinance on themselves particularly if these towns form at present most attractive growth centers therein [Vepa, 1968: 493].

If this rigorous control of industrial locations by licensing is economically undesirable and "politically hazardous," apart from being "negative" in its approach, it would seem that some kind of guidance and regulations would still be necessary in order to direct industries away from the overcongested big cities to other suitable locations, and to create the necessary environment in the prospective growth points to attract private industrialists to these areas.[25]

However, as the discussions in the preceding sections indicate, from the appropriateness and sufficiency of the definition of the term "urban," to the nature, extent, and direction of the urban industrial relationship, to the role of occupational structure as indicator of urban and economic development in the developing countries—a consensus is yet to be reached among the scholars in India and abroad. The urban-industrial pattern in India, with the disproportionate growth of larger urban centers, an excessive concentration of population and industries in a few select places, and the resultant regional and urban-rural imbalances, suggests that a concerted and decisive action must be taken to control these problems. Efforts that have been made in this direction are laudable from the point of view of the almost insurmountable difficulties that had to be faced by the planners and administrators in a newly independent country with her teeming millions and a weak industrial base. But the fact remains that the measures taken have not been totally successful and the problems facing rural and urban life in India today are as great as ever.

One immediate course of action in this regard points toward the need fo more research as to the causes, concomitants, and consequences of urbanization and urban growth. More empirical knowledge and information on the factors associated with, or determinants of, urbanization are needed to enable the planners and policymakers to control and rechannel the untoward pattern of urban development. In the following sections we propose to take an exploratory step toward this direction.

URBANIZATION-INDUSTRIALIZATION DYNAMICS

The broad spectrum of complex relationships between urbanization and economic development, or more particularly industrialization, has long intrigued social scientists. However, this very complexity has led researchers to use methods which are as multidimensional as the goals sought and the relationships to be explored. Methods have varied from simple descriptive studies to rigorous statistical analyses; goals, from inquiries into the existence of any relationship between urban and industrial growth to measurements of the contribution and interaction of the multitude of intricate forces that make up the developmental processes. Definitions and indices used in these inquiries have differed considerably, whereby a phenomenon having the same popular connotation has been measured by various indices by different researchers.[26] Before probing into India's pattern of development, we present the following brief review in order to illustrate the divergent nature of research which relates to the present work.

RELATED RESEARCH

With the proportion of population residing in cities of 100,000 and above as an index of the degree of urbanization, and the proportion of economically-occupied males in nonagricultural pursuits as an index of industrialization, and taking the "countries and territories of the world" as units, Davis and Golden (1957: 122), have noted a high positive correlation (.86) between urbanization and industrialization. In the context of India's rapid urbanization, Davis (1951) considered rural-urban migration spurred by increased economic opportunity as a leading cause of urban growth, and hypothesized that, in this situation, cities with higher levels of industrialization would grow more rapidly than others. By taking 37 cities classified by proportion of workers in manufacturing, and then in manufacturing, trade, and transport combined, he found support for his hypothesis (Davis, 1951: 137).

However, Bose (as cited in Hoselitz, 1960b: 362-363) in his 1956 study found no significant difference in the growth rate of industrial as compared with administrative centers. On the basis of the National Sample Survey data, D. K. Bose (1969) found a correlation of .58 between degree of urbanization and industrialization (proportion of labor force in manufacturing) in India. Upon further analysis, Bose (1969: 1169) noted that

> contrary to popular expectations, no association between overall rate of urbanization (as defined by the proportion of total population living in urban areas) and the level of industrialization in the economy as indicated by the proportion of work force engaged in mining and manufacturing industries, can be clearly established. On the other hand, a good measure of relationship between urbanization and industrialization can be found when the medium-sized towns, with population between 20,000 and 50,000 are considered separately. The relationship is found to be weakest in respect of bigger towns and cities with population of 100,000 and above.

Basu (1965) compared the coefficients of urbanization and coefficients of industrialization for the states of India, 1961, and noted that "states which show a higher coefficient of urbanization simultaneously show a higher coefficient of industrialization" (1965: 25).

On a world perspective, Wilkinson (1960), using statistics for the period around 1950, studied 49 nations to investigate the relationship between level of industrialization and metropolitanization. He found a correlation (r) or .776 between the index of metropolitanization (percent of population in metropolitan areas/percent of population defined urban) and industrialization (percent males in nonagricultural employment) and came to the conclusion that—even though earlier studies had shown a close association between industrial development and the extent of urbanization or the proportion of population residing in cities—"the concentration or depth of urbanization as measured by the ratio of metropolitan population to administratively defined urban population, does not correlate as closely with economic development." He suggested that "the source of this divergence lies in the fact that metropolitan growth is heavily influenced by the structure of the industrialization process, not by industrialization as such alone" (Wilkinson, 1960: 362-363). He also noted that with an increase in the extent of urbanization, with some exceptions, (including India) the association between industrialization and metropolitanization becomes closer (1960: 357-359).

In a similar, but more extensive, study of metropolitan growth for between 68 and 78 countries and territories of the world ("the number varying according to the independent variable and the index of growth") accounting for 81–85% of the total metropolitan areas of the world, Gibbs and Schnore (1960: 169) found that "the greater the industrialization [measured in this study by per capita energy consumption], the higher the degree of metropolitanization; the higher the degree of metropolitanization, in turn, the lower the rate of metropolitan growth and the greater the proportion of the national increase that accrues to metropolitan areas."

In all but the last of the above studies, the investigators used nonagricultural employment as an indicator of industrialization. At this point it may be noted parenthetically that throughout the literature the term "economic development" has been interchangeably used with "industrialization" or "industrial development" and "modernization."[27] This interchangeable use of the terms, as Weller and Sly (1969: 314) have indicated, may be "primarily . . . for stylistic convenience, and because in the long run economic development, particularly if it is brought about by industrialization, implies modernization. Moreover, practically all countries that currently are economically developed are also modernized in the sociological sense of the word." In keeping with this flexibility of definitions, in a number of studies, indicators or correlates of economic development, modernization, and industrialization, other than industrial employment have been used as measures of these phenomena. Hauser (1959: 99) discussed "some of the demographic measurements which may have utility as indicators of economic development," and along with some other indicators of economic development (such as per capita income, percentage of gross national product derived from agriculture, and percentage of labor force employed in agriculture), tested their usefulness on 13 selected countries. The research revealed, among other findings, that some of the demographic rates, including the "percentage of population urban," were "poor predictors of the economic measurements used" (Hauser, 1959: 116).

Aiming "to present some recent data on the relationship of selected demographic measures to levels of economic development," Stockwell (1966) grouped 49 countries according to their per capita income in U.S. dollars and computed correlation coefficients (rho) between economic development (as indicated by per capita income) and twelve demographic measures, including two measures of urbanization (20,000 and over, and 100,000 and over). He found that

in both cases, the degree of urbanization is positively correlated with level of economic development, with the association being slightly more pronounced for the proportion of population living in places of 100,000 or more (r = .41) than for the proportion of places of 20,000 or more (r = .35). Thus, although the association is less pronounced than it is for most of the other demographic measures here considered, these data would suggest that the extent of population concentration continues to be a meaningful indicator of the level of economic development [Stockwell, 1966: 220].

On a broader base, using a range of 94-123 nations and taking per capita energy consumption as the indicator of modernization, Weller and Sly (1969) attempted to analyze the relationship between six demographic variables and modernization through rank-order correlation techniques. They noted that the data indicated modernization to be "a good indicator of relative levels of demographic behavior, and these variables have shown a moderately high association at specified periods through time," but cautioned against any broad generalization, as "even for relatively narrow range of energy consumption there is a wide range of demographic behavior" (Weller and Sly, 1969: 322).

By taking percentage of total population in urban areas of over 20,000 as the index of urbanization, and per capita income as that of economic development for 72 countries (mid-1950s), Friedmann and Lackington (1967: 7) found a correlation (r) of .69 at .001 level of significance, noted a disequilibrium between the levels of urbanization and per capita income of some countries, and suggested that societies showing such disparity are "likely to experience serious internal tensions."

In the context of testing the thesis of over-urbanization, Kamerschen (1969) conducted a multivariate statistical analysis for 80 countries of the world. Using urbanization (percentage of population in cities of 20,000 and over, and a measure of primacy), industrialization (percentage in nonagricultural occupations), four land density measures, and per capita income as variables—he found a high correlation between per capita income, industrialization, and urbanization in the underdeveloped countries. His most pertinent conclusion in this context was that "there is no significantly closer (positive) relationship between industrialization and urbanization in all countries, or more especially developed countries, than in the underdeveloped countries" (Kamerschen, 1969: 246).

In another study Gibbs and Martin (1962) have examined the relationship between the degree of urbanization and such variables as "dispersion of object of consumption," "division of labor," and "levels of technological development," and high correlations among the variables led these researchers to remark that: "Just as it is necessary for the populations of large cities to draw objects of consumption from greater distances so is it equally necessary for them to have a high degree of division of labor and technological development to accomplish the task" (Gibbs and Martin, 1962: 674).

Schnore (1963) considered a number of variables as indicators of modernization and urbanization in an attempt to further the understanding of the "correlates of urbanization." Unlike most previous research, his consideration of a cluster of variables (indicators of modernization) other than industrial is based on the conviction of the existence of other measurable correlates of urbanization. Based on rank-order correlation techniques, Schnore's analysis showed a high coefficient between most variables of modernization and two measures of urbanization (a yield between .50 and .90 in eighteen out of a total of twenty). The correlation matrix among the variables revealed a generally high and positive correlation with the exception of one variable. Schnore's research provided valuable insights on aspects of the interrelationships between urbanization and economic development as he undertook further statistical analysis (factor analysis) to confirm the significance of the association between the above variables and urbanization.

Among the noneconomic factors, literacy (along with its concomitants such as number of scholars or educational institutions) have long been considered associated with urban-industrial development, and a number of descriptive and empirical studies have noted an association or correlation between these two. Golden (1955), for example, found a correlation (r) of .87 and .84 between literacy and industrialization as measured by "proportion of gainfully occupied males in nonagricultural pursuits" and by per capita income respectively. She considered literacy an "index of socioeconomic development" and noted that "the differential rates of economic advance for the educationally retarded and the educationally advanced countries point to the importance of the dissemination of literacy and education in the transformation of peasant-agricultural nations into urban-industrial nations" (Golden, 1955: 6).

In the Indian context, Gosal (1964), after a descriptive analysis of the spatial pattern of literacy, stated that "high rates of literacy are also strongly correlated to a high degree of urbanization and agricultural prosperity." Kamerschen (1968), however, "called into question" the Golden thesis and—on the basis of his detailed statistical study of 80 countries divided in two groups according to per capita income in U.S. dollars—wrote:

the major positive conclusion of the study is that the data seem to support a "threshold" (discrete) theory or index rather than a "continuous" theory as suggested by Golden. That is, the index seems to work up to a certain level of socioeconomic development and after that either works in the opposite direction or becomes indiscriminating [Kamerschen, 1968: 175].

The brief review above supports Schnore's criticism of the one-factor approach prevalent in the literature. As Schnore (1963: 231-232) has pointed out, most researchers have sought the relationship between one factor with all others and very seldom have made any attempt toward "simultaneously ascertaining the manifold associations among a large number of indicators of modernization." He maintained that

> the major conclusion to be drawn from these materials, however, is that the linkage assumed between industrialization and urbanization —valid though it may be in a gross way—represent a simplistic view. In point of fact, "there are a number of variables that show equivalent degrees of association with urbanization." This is not a denial of the possibility that many of these other indices are themselves concomitants or consequences of industrialization. It is a plea, however, for the recognition of the many facets of the topic that are likely to be overlooked by focusing exclusive attention upon industrialization in the limited sense of industrial structure. Certainly, other organizational features and technological, environmental and demographic traits as well, warrant attention in any full-scale analysis of the subject [Schnore, 1963: 235].

UNIT OF STUDY

In the federal constitutional system, India is a union of states and union territories. Local governments, such as municipalities, town committees, union boards, and other local bodies, are created by the states and power is granted to such local bodies to function effectively. Therefore states have the potential to play a vital role in solving complex urban problems of regional and local nature through guidance, delegation of power, or the necessary administrative set-up for effective planning and implementation of urbanization policy. Moreover, states are organized primarily on the basis of distinctive cultural and linguistic patterns. Considering the uniqueness of each state and its responsibilities, it was considered that the state as a unit of study for the project would be meaningful.

Certain problems of concentration of population and industrial activities in larger urban units and in some states, have been discussed earlier. In view of India's present developmental planning schemes with particular reference to the problems of the creation and distribution of resources, and the accomplishment of an urbanization policy (and the availability of data by states on various aspects of urban and industrial development), it was thought that within the scope of our objectives an investigation utilizing the state as a unit of study would contribute to the understanding of patterns within a broad regional framework.

Also, in view of the importance of centers of over 100,000 in shaping the urban and economic patterns of India, and due to the availability of comparable data for this size group, cities of India were also taken as units of study in a further analysis of urban growth.

EXPLANATORY VARIABLES

Availability of data has necessarily been a major factor in the selection of variables for the present study. A number of variables deemed to be highly appropriate had to be foregone for lack of adequate data. Among the available variables, selection has been guided by the relevant literature and the expectation that, individually or collectively, directly or indirectly, these variables might be associated with the urbanization pattern of India for the period under study.

A detailed description of the nature and source of each of the variables is presented in the Appendix. They can, for the sake of convenience, be grouped into six categories: urban, industrial, developmental, educational, demographic, and spatial. (The groupings are quite subjective; per capita income and electricity consumption, for example, could probably be included within the industrial category rather than the developmental.)

As has been emphasized time and again by scholars in this field, urbanization, as measured by proportional increase of urban to total population, and urban growth, measured as an increase in the absolute number of the urban populace, are two different phenomena. The contributing and consequential factors of urban growth and urbanization may or may not be the same; factors contributing to an increase in the absolute number of urban population over a period, for example, may not have the same effect with respect to the proportional change of urban to total population. Considerations such as these have prompted us to view the dependent variables from three different perspectives: degree of urbanization (urban population as proportion of the total state population), urbanization change (proportional change in urban population), and urban growth or percentage variation (urban population change in 1951-1961 as percentage of 1951).

In order to ascertain whether the nature and magnitude of the association between the dependent and independent variables would vary according to the size of urban places, degree of urbanization in the six urban size classes, and urban growth and urbanization in the three largest size groups were also taken as dependent variables.

Industrial

Among the basic causes and consequences of urbanization or urban growth, industrialization as indicated by the structure or growth of the industrial labor force may be a factor of highest importance. Although an association of urbanization with development in the secondary and tertiary sectors of the economy is clear, the relative weight and nature of such associations are still matters of investigation and research. Hence, industrialization, both static and over time, is hypothesized to be the foremost independent variable in this study of urban phenomena in India. Among the possible indicators of industrialization—such as industrial output, productivity per worker, and so forth—workers in the nonagricultural categories are taken as industrial indices, both on account of ready availability and the potential for comparability in crosscultural research at an international scale.

The same logic that suggested calculating the urban variables in three forms (degree of urbanization, urban growth, and urbanization change) prevailed in compiling the data on industrial variables. These variables are made up of male workers (being more representative of the labor force of India) in nonagricultural industrial categories. Over the decade 1951-1961, industrialization (proportional) has remained almost stagnant or has actually declined in some instances, while industrial growth (absolute number) has increased in almost all the states. Hence, for an appropriate assessment of the role of industry on urbanization and urban growth phenomena, industrial data in various employment categories were calculated as (1) a proportion of state total population, (2) a proportion of total male workers, and (3) as percentage variation.

Developmental

Ever since the dawn of urbanism in the post-Industrial Revolution era in the West, an association between urbanization and economic development has gradually come into focus. In order to establish the nature and degree of such association, researchers have taken a vast array of variables under consideration. The nature of such variables, however, differs according to the economic and cultural background of the nation concerned. Number of private cars, refrigerators, and cooking ranges, for example, though acceptable as probable yardsticks relating economic development or standard of living among the more developed countries, would not be very discriminating in the context of a developing country such as India, where these are luxury items possessed by only a small fraction of the total population.

Variables included in this category for the present study have consequently been selected more as symbolic of the various facets of developmental efforts undertaken in independent India than as standard developmental variables that are found in the literature. Briefly: post offices symbolize communication; surfaced roads and motor vehicles (since they incorporate both private, public, and goods vehicles) indicate level of transportation of goods and services; hospitals typify the efforts to improve health standards; per capita income and electricity consumption very grossly represent the standard of living; and net domestic production and income from nonagricultural sectors in each state may be considered as indicative of its level of economic development. It is believed that the developmental level of a state would be reflected in the level of urbanization and vice versa, and the degree of such association will be worthwhile to estimate.

Educational

As the current literature on urban phenomena suggests, an attempt to account for urbanization with only selected industrial and developmental factors as independent variables (but without acknowledging the role of cultural or educational factors) would be rather incomplete. Furthermore, since it is found that higher educational attainment is more prevalent among urban dwellers, the question that prompted selection of the three variables in this category is whether educational level of a state would be associated with the degree of urbanization. The variables selected for this purpose reflect educational level in India from three dimensions: namely, a basic literacy rate, a higher standard of education ranging from primary to highly professional education, and a population-educational institution ratio. Considering the extremes in the Indian educational scene, ranging from the about 65% illiterates to the highly sophisticated and professionally educated minority, a combination of these three variables was thought to be more appropriate than any one of them or some other variable indicating scholars in specific branches of higher learning.

Demographic

Migration, natural increase of population in urban places, the age-sex composition of urban dwellers, and so on, are some of the basic variables commonly employed in analyses of urbanization. In the study of Indian patterns, due to limited access to precise demographic data, three general variables—namely, natural increase, variation in population size, and interstate migration and immigration from abroad—are taken as independent variables in the analysis. That labor migrates from one region to another to avail itself of employment opportunities is clear, but how far the flow of state-to-state migration in India is associated with the urban pattern and growth is yet to be explored. However, as it is estimated that of the total interstate migrants about 61.4% move to the urban areas of other states (Sen Gupta and Sdasyuk, 1968: 81), it seems reasonable that interstate migration should have some association with urbanization.

Spatial

Location relative to large cities and change in the areal size of urban centers are considered to be responsible, to a certain extent, for urban growth. In order to assess their contribution, distance to the "million" cities, as well as to cities of 100,000 population and over, and the change in areal size are taken as independent variables in the analysis of city growth.

DATA: SOURCE AND PROBLEMS

As a source of data, heavy reliance has been placed on the census reports, particularly the post-census monographs. Census Paper No. 1 of 1962 and Census Paper No. 1 of 1967 have especially been useful in that they provided adjusted data on industrial workers which could be used for comparative purposes. Publication by the Central Statistical Organization (CSO) and by the National Council of Applied Economic Research (NCAER) have also provided some of the necessary data for the analyses (for details, see Appendix).

In going through the census reports of a newly independent developing country with a vast population like India, one is awed by their detailed and multidimensional nature. From "economic and demographic to ethnographic and descriptive" (Stoner, 1965), the 1961 census has provided a wide variety of facts and figures, making it vastly superior to the previous censuses in both coverage and techniques. However, from the point of view of usefulness of the data for any systematic research, investigators are faced with certain problems, some of which are common to other national surveys of this nature. Stoner (1965: 17) encompasses some of these problems in a nutshell when he states

The dynamic character of a Census' content from decade to decade poses problems of spatial and temporal analysis. Such events as changing boundaries, of enumeration areas, redefinition of components (such as the industrial or occupational parameters of the term "urban") or the inclusion or exclusion of data are common faults resulting from revisions intended to produce more meaningful surveys.

In one form or other, most of these problems have cropped up in the course of the present research.

Changes in definitions and concepts have posed a major obstacle in the comparability of 1951 and 1961 data. Change in the definition of "urban" has been discussed in an earlier section. Change in the definitions of industrial categories had made it virtually impossible to compare the 1951 and 1961 industrial workers, if not for the adjusted data published in the Census Papers No. 1 and No. 7. Even then, the change in the concept of economic classification has, as the post-census Paper was quick to point out, "rendered proper allocation of past censuses sometimes difficult" (*Census of India, 1961,* 1962: XXV; Mahajan, 1965: 12). The 1951 classification was based on a person's occupation regardless of the industry he was employed in. The 1961 census, on the other hand, classified the worker according to industry (*Census of India, 1961,* 1962: XXV). Thus, even with the adjusted data, any interpretation of the findings would have to be mixed with caution.

Certain ambiguities and inconsistencies in the presentation of data in the census have been noted in the course of this work. The category of "household industry" in 1961, for example, has been carved out of the "production other than cultivation" category of 1951. In the adjusted data for the industrial workers, therefore, the column for category IV, household industry, is kept blank in 1951; while the next column, category V, indicates the data for "manufacturing other than household industry" in both 1951 and 1961. It would be logical therefore to assume that category V ("manufacturing other than household industry") in 1951 would be comparable to that of 1961. However, as statement 23 of Paper No. 1 of 1962 indicates: category V of 1951 would, according to the census, be actually comparable to the 1961 categories IV and V combined. Excerpts from statement 23 and from two tables of industrial workers' data from the same publication illustrate this confusing situation (*Census of India, 1961,* 1962: XXVIII, 406-407, 412-413).[28]

Statement 23: Variation in the percentage of male workers at (a) Household Industry (category IV) and (b) in Manufacturing other than Household Industry (category V), 1951-1961

State/Union Territory	1951 Percentage	1961 Percentage (IV + V)	Difference
All India	9.84	5.71 + 5.56 = 11.27	+1.43

Tables 11-C (1951) and 12C (1961): Percentage distribution of male workers into industrial categories in different states of India, 1951, 1961

State/Union Territory	Total Workers	At Household Industry	Manufacturing other than Household Ind.
1951	100	———	9.86
1961	100	5.71	5.56

A late discovery of these inconsistencies required repeated computation for a number of analyses with inevitable wastage of researchers' and computer time.[29]

Even though the topical coverage of the 1961 census far exceeded that of any other previous census, and the publications by the CSO, NCAER, and some regional statistical organizations provided a wealth of facts and figures, a uniform presentation of detailed data in certain areas—particularly those regarding urban centers of different size classes—is still to be achieved. Dearth of data on the emigration and natural increase of population in urban places during the 1951-1961 intercensal period and detailed data on industrial workers in individual towns are some of the lacunae among the otherwise colossal accumulation of materials of the Indian census that have been painfully noticeable during this research.

Also, there are still some crucial gaps in the information, particularly on the behavioral and social aspects, data on which are almost nonexistent at the present time. In the context of developmental and social change towards modernizing Indian society, not all the related questions need to be necessarily economic in nature. For example, satisfactory answers to the fundamental issue—what measures should be adopted to check the rural-urban migration and natural increase of population—must await more information and relevant data on a wide range of sociocultural, political, and spatial variables, such as cultural mores, adaptiveness, motivation, and so forth, along with the geographical distribution of resources to assess local and regional potentials for development.[30]

Finally, the traditional "word of caution." Inaccuracy and unreliability in Indian statistics, (Asthana and Srivastava, 1965: chs. 1 and 3; Schwartzberg, 1969: 29-42), particularly in the earlier census reports, were due partly to collection of data by untrained personnel and partly to ambiguity and complications in the census questions. Although some of these sources of error were eradicated to a large extent in the 1961 census through personnel training, clarification and simplification of questions, and so on, certain reservations must still be made regarding the data. The following statement, although perhaps rather too pessimistic, provides an example relevant to the present study:

The fundamental characteristic of occupational classification of India has been that like other Census details it relates to one day only and as such due caution must be exercised while drawing any inference from it. In India an individual follows a 'number of occupations simultaneously and even he himself does not know which particular occupation is his main or subsidiary. All this renders the collected data highly fluctuating and non-comparable [Asthana and Srivastava, 1965: 105].

However, in spite of these problems with the data and the adjustments that were necessary to mold the data for analytical purposes, it is believed that the published figures were adequate for this research project. It is hoped that the next census will be more precise, and more comparable to the current one than the 1961 census, with all its changes, has been to the previous census; and a more detailed and sophisticated follow-up analysis with the forthcoming census data could be built on the basic premises set forth in this study.

STATIC AND DYNAMIC MODELS: EMERGING PATTERNS

In order to assess the relative importance of the various factors that influenced the process of urbanization during the 1951-1961 decade, a series of stepwise multiple regression models were undertaken. Basically, the models differ according to the purpose of analysis—that is, some are static, others dynamic. Models I-a and I-b are static models (1961), which attempt (in the first) to account for the proportion of the population of states that is urban, and (in the second) the proportion of the population in various urban size classes in the states, respectively. The dynamic models, 2-a, 2-b, and 2-c, seek to account for the change in urban growth and urbanization for states and for various urban size classes as a result of change in certain economic, cultural, developmental, and demographic conditions.

Our knowledge of the contemporary situation in India, and the patterns of other developing countries have led us to postulate a number of general hypotheses: the degree of urbanization of a state should be related to its occupational level in the secondary and tertiary sectors, and also to its overall cultural and developmental level; and the proportion of population in the larger urban places should have a strong relationship with the industrial, cultural, and demographic variables, whereas the smaller places should be highly correlated with developmental variables. Percentage variation of labor force in manufacturing and construction, in the three categories in the tertiary sector (especially in the "other services"), along with the demographic variables, should be significantly related to urban growth; but because of the broader base of population and higher rate of natural increase, the relationship between proportional change in the dependent and independent variables should be less pronounced.

MODEL I-a: Static Analysis (1961: 15 states and 7 union territories)

> *Dependent variable:* Percentage urban in 15 states and 7 union territories.

> *Independent variables:* Expressed as proportion of the state population.

>> *Industrial:* The following variables indicate male workers in various industrial categories: nonagricultural (secondary and tertiary combined); secondary; tertiary.

>> *Cultural:* Literacy; educational institutions; scholars.

>> *Developmental:* Motor vehicles; establishments; hospitals; surfaced roads.

>> *Demographic:* 1951-1961 net variation in population; 1951-1961 net increase/decrease by internal migration and emigration; 1951-1961 natural increase of population.

> *Highest simple r's were:*

establishments	.935
tertiary	.919
nonagricultural	.843

The only significant variables (at the .05 level) were establishments and employment in the tertiary sector, but the R^2 was very high: .953. It appears that the proportion urban by state more closely reflects general commercialization and the level of tertiary activities than industrialization.

MODEL I-b: Static Analysis (1961: 15 states)

> *Dependent variables:* Percentage of population in Classes I, II, III, IV, V, and VI. Each of the dependent variables is taken individually in problems 1 through 6.

> *Independent variables:* Expressed as proportion of the state population.

>> *Industrial:* The following variables indicate male workers in various industrial categories: nonagricultural; secondary; tertiary.

>> *Cultural:* Literacy; educational institutions; scholars.

Developmental: Motor vehicles; post offices; establishments; hospitals; surfaced roads; per capita electricity consumption; per capita income.

Demographic: 1951-1961 net variation in population; 1951-1961 net increase/decrease by internal migration and emigration; 1951-1961 natural increase of population.

Problem I-b.1: Class I centers (100,000 and over): $R^2 = .92$

Highest r's:		
	establishments	.911
	secondary	.771
	electricity consumption	.559

Significant variables were establishments, per capita electricity consumption, and literacy; but workers in the secondary sector were highly intercorrelated (.77 with the dependent variable, .70 with establishments). Employment in the secondary sector was more important to the Class I centers than to the other size groups, but still the proportion of the population in these large places appears to be dependent upon a mixture of industrial, commercial, and cultural development variables.

Problem I-b.2: Class II centers (50,000-99,999): $R^2 = .88$

Highest r's:		
	per capita income	.811
	post offices	.780
	literacy	.740
	nonagricultural	.704
	secondary	.667

Significant variables were per capita income and post offices. Class II centers as a group are less dependent on commercial activities than were Class I centers, but more on nonagricultural opportunities generally, including moderate dependence on industrial activities and on public services such as post offices. These centers tend to have the highest per capita income and literacy.

Problem I-b.3: Class III centers (20,000-49,999): $R^2 = .92$

Highest r's:		
	post offices	.759
	per capita income	.721
	nonagricultural	.707
	secondary	.662

Significant variables were post offices and establishments. Class III centers (like Class II) depend on nonagricultural employment generally (moderately on secondary) and public services (e.g., post offices); but like Class I centers, on commerce (establishments) as well. Class III centers also have relatively good income and a fairly high level of literacy.

Problem I-b.4: Class IV centers (10,000-19,999): $R^2 = .78$

| *Highest r's:* | surfaced roads | .798 |
| | secondary | .691 |

Significant variables included the above, together with natural increase of population. Class IV centers may perhaps be interpreted as reflecting the general level of development (roads, for example), but these also show some dependence on the secondary sector. Many of these towns are located near large metropolises or at transport nodes.

Problem I-b.5: Class V centers (5,000-9,999): $R^2 = .50$

| *Highest r's:* | hospitals | .649 |
| | establishments | .420 |

Significant variables were hospitals and roads. Results are weak, indicating the need for other explanatory variables. However, Class V centers seem mainly to be local service centers.

Problem I-b.6: Class VI centers (below 5,000): $R^2 = .63$

| *Highest r's:* | natural increase | −.598 |
| | migration | .571 |

Significant variables were natural increase and migration. These smallest centers are associated with low income and low natural increase, but with some in-migration (possibly indicative of the "step-migration" in recent years). However, results are somewhat weak and inconclusive.

The level of urbanization in 1961, particularly in the urban centers over 10,000, does reflect levels of secondary employment, but that the relation is no greater than that with tertiary activity may not be surprising in view of the fact that, in India as a whole, tertiary employment is almost twice as large as secondary employment (see Table 2 above), and that many places exist as local service centers.

Three versions of a dynamic model were tested: (2-a), in which change was measured as the percentage variation—i.e., percentage increase or decrease over the 1951 base; (2-b), in which change was simply the difference between the 1951 and 1961 urban percentage of the total population; and (2-c), as in (2-b), but with the industrial variables calculated as a proportion of male workers, rather than of total population. The latter (2-c) results were generally less satisfactory. Rather than report all results, we discuss for each size group studied, the version (2-a, 2-b, or 2-c) which was more successful. The units of study for each of these three models were fourteen states of India (excluding Jammu and Kashmir).

MODEL 2-a: Dynamic (1951-1961)

Dependent variables: Percentage variation in total urban population, and in Classes I, II, and III urban places, respectively.

Independent variables:

Industrial: Unless otherwise indicated, the following variables reflect percentage variation of male workers in the various industrial categories: household and manufacturing; construction; trade and commerce; transport, storage and communication; other services; nonagricultural; male and female in nonagricultural.

Developmental: Percentage variation of state income in nonagricultural sectors; percentage change in per capita income.

Demographic: Net variation in population; net increase/decrease by internal migration and emigration; natural increase.

MODEL 2-b: Dynamic (1951-1961)

Dependent variables: Difference in the proportion urban, and in Classes I, II, and III urban centers respectively.

Independent variables:

Industrial: Unless otherwise indicated, the following variables reflect change in the percentage of male workers in the various industrial categories to total population: household and manufacturing; trade and commerce; transport, storage and communications; other services; nonagricultural; male and female in nonagricultural.

Developmental: Change in percentage distribution of net domestic product in nonagricultural sectors; percentage change in per capita income; change in the annual per capita consumption of electricity.

Demographic: Net variation in population; net increase/decrease by internal migration and emigration; natural increase.

MODEL 2-c: Dynamic (1951-1961)

This is identical to 2-b, except that in this model the industrial variables were expressed as change in the percentage of male industrial workers to total male workers.

Problem 2.1: State urban population: R^2 = .88

Highest r's:		
	net domestic product	.580
	other services	.572
	male and female nonagricultural	.528
	nonagricultural	.510

For this problem, 2-a results were best. Significant variables were change in other services, net domestic product, and transport, storage and communication. During the decade 1951-1961, urban growth seemed mainly to be dependent on growth of tertiary employment of various kinds, rather than on industrialization (secondary sector).

Problem 2.2: Class I centers: $R^2 = .50$

   Highest r: transport, storage and communication   .610

In this problem, the 2-c version, though poor, was best. However, results were contradictory and not too meaningful. An inverse relation with change in nonagricultural employment may indicate that Class I centers did less well than other size groups, or that urban growth continued despite a lack of opportunities in either secondary or tertiary activities. Clearly, other variables are needed to account for change in the large places.

Problem 2.3: Class II centers $R^2 = .39$

   Highest r: trade and commerce $-.460$

Results in the 2-a version, though poor, were best for this problem. Most important variables were clearly not included, but apparently centers depending on trade grew more slowly, and those dependent on other services grew more rapidly.

Problem 2.4: Class III centers: $R^2 = .88$

   Highest r's: transport, storage and communication $-.734$
                    other services   .585

In this problem, the 2-b version gave the best results. Significant variables included change in transport, storage and communication, manufacturing, and trade and commerce. Class III centers appear to have grown in inverse relation to the change in transport employment, but in direct relation to growth in other secondary and tertiary employment.

Problem 2.5: Classes I, II, and III centers combined: $R^2 = .59$

   Highest r's: male and female, nonagricultural   .522
                    nonagricultural   .498
                    trade and commerce   .438
                    per capita income   .437
                    manufacturing   .422

In this problem too, version 2-b gave best results. Significant variables were change in male and female nonagricultural employment, natural increase of population, and change in the net domestic product in the nonagricultural sectors. Again, change during the decade was associated more with change in nonagricultural employment generally, than with secondary activity specifically.

General Assessment of Residuals

Residual maps are increasingly utilized for gaining a deeper understanding of spatial deviation in patterns of a particular phenomenon under study.[31] In the present study, residuals from some of the relatively more successful regression models have been plotted (Figure 6), so that additional variables that might be useful could be considered for further analyses of urbanization in India.

The map for Model 2-a (urban growth) shows a wide range of scores varying from 30.62 to −15.67. On the basis of the selected variables, urban growth for the decade in Assam, Orissa, and Madhya Pradesh was significantly underestimated; whereas in Bihar and Mysore it was overestimated.

In Model 1-b, static analysis, the map for Class I cities shows a pattern in which urbanization was overestimated in Punjab and underestimated in Maharashtra. Except in Bihar, Orissa, and Assam, the maps for Classes II and III urban centers indicate an almost analogous spatial pattern of both over and underestimation. Although, due to a great deal of spatial variation of negative and positive scores, no definite regional patterns emerge in these maps, it is to be noted that the magnitude of variations among the states appears to be small.

A close examination of the residual maps—along with the spatial distribution of major minerals and power plants, urban population, and density of the transportation network—suggests a number of factors affecting urbanization in India at the static level or through time. The states differ significantly in physical resource endowments, transportation networks, level of resource utilization, and availability of entrepreneurial skills needed to inspire the people toward achieving the developmental goals. These factors might have contributed toward the unexplained variations in the regression models. Therefore, the results of analyses, although revealing, clearly indicate the necessity of additional variables related to the above for a systematic and logical model construction.

In view of the above, the following variables are deemed to be worth considering for future analyses:

(1) Degree of urban population, 1951: This variable could have an important bearing as the higher urban status of some states in 1951 might

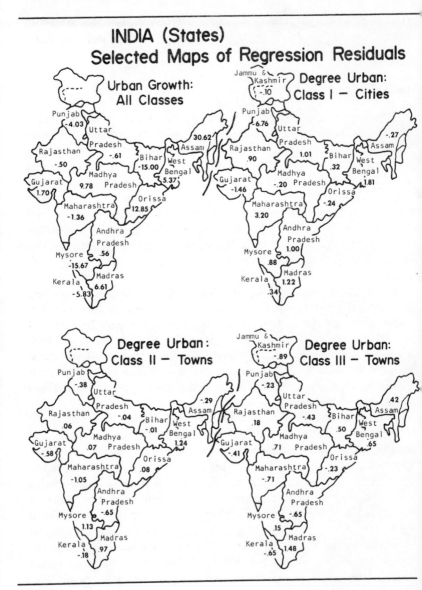

INDIA (States)
Selected Maps of Regression Residuals

Urban Growth: All Classes

Punjab -4.03
Uttar Pradesh -.61
Rajasthan -.50
Bihar -15.00
Assam 30.62
West Bengal 5.37
Gujarat 1.70
Madhya Pradesh 9.78
Orissa 12.85
Maharashtra -1.36
Andhra Pradesh .56
Mysore -15.67
Madras 6.61
Kerala -5.83

Degree Urban: Class I — Cities

Jammu & Kashmir -.10
Punjab -6.76
Uttar Pradesh 1.01
Rajasthan .90
Bihar .32
Assam -.27
West Bengal 1.81
Gujarat -1.46
Madhya Pradesh -.20
Orissa -.24
Maharashtra 3.20
Andhra Pradesh 1.00
Mysore .88
Madras 1.22
Kerala .34

Degree Urban: Class II — Towns

Punjab -.38
Uttar Pradesh -.04
Rajasthan .06
Bihar -.01
Assam -.29
West Bengal 1.24
Gujarat -.58
Madhya Pradesh .07
Orissa .08
Maharashtra -1.05
Andhra Pradesh -.65
Mysore 1.13
Madras .97
Kerala -.18

Degree Urban: Class III — Towns

Jammu & Kashmir -.89
Punjab -.23
Uttar Pradesh -.43
Rajasthan .18
Bihar .50
Assam .42
West Bengal .65
Gujarat -.41
Madhya Pradesh .71
Orissa -.23
Maharashtra -.71
Andhra Pradesh -.65
Mysore .15
Madras 1.48
Kerala -.65

Figure 6.

have an added impact on the urbanization process by attracting (with large external economies, urban amenities, and so forth) or, conversely, by discouraging (congestion, competition in job market, and so on) migration into the urban areas. Interestingly, in the residual map for Class I cities, the states with the highest degree of urbanization in 1951 (e.g., West Bengal, Madras, Mysore, Gujarat, Punjab) are located at both extremes of the scale, possibly indicating an influence of the degree of urban population in 1951 on that of 1961.

(2) Resource endowments: A quantified assessment of mineral resources for the states in light of their potentials for development would probably yield more information concerning urbanization. Many of the relatively less urbanized states (Rajasthan, Madhya Pradesh, Orissa, and Assam, for example) whose urbanization was generally underestimated are rich in exploitable minerals and are beginning to utilize such resources; some others are deficient in mineral resources, but are developing the "agro-based" and "nonresource-based" engineering industries. These factors could help to account for the underestimations of the dependent variables as shown in the residual maps.

Energy production nodes also play a key role in the establishment of certain industries, particularly in the mineral-rich states (previously unexploited), which might promote urbanization in such states. Therefore, level of power production may be a significant factor in assessing urbanization.

(3) Transport network: The importance of traffic structure in the establishment and development of industries and services should be given due consideration in the analyses of urbanization. In a developing economy like that of India, a transport network assumes a special role in the spatial development of production of goods and services and the creation of distribution centers. States such as West Bengal, Maharashtra, and Madras with larger metropolitan centers and seaports have better transport facilities than other "interior" (Madhya Pradesh) or "frontier" (Assam) states. But the share of transport network (both roads and railways) in the development process has increased significantly, particularly in regard to strategically located states in terms of potential raw material resources or from political considerations. Although one variable in this category (surfaced roads) has been taken under consideration for the analyses, density of railways (as over 70% of the freight traffic load is carried by railways), along with unsurfaced road density, might be variables related to urbanization.

(4) Capital investment: The size of investment both in public and private sectors provides necessary input in the developmental patterns which in turn might be associated with urbanization. States with exploitable mineral resources or those already at a higher level of industrial development could attract more investment than other states. Therefore, some measure of investment—per capita investment, for example—may be considered as a variable in the study of urbanization.

It may also be noted here that changes in status of some of the rural centers as a result of census reclassification of towns in 1961 are also likely to partially explain urban growth at least in a few states. In some of the states where urban growth was most highly underestimated, emergence of new towns accounted for a large proportion of urban growth (e.g., Assam: 56%, Orissa: 59%, and Madhya Pradesh: 40%).

GROWTH OF CITIES: AN OVERVIEW[32]

In view of the role played by the larger centers in shaping the urban pattern of India, an analysis was undertaken to determine the association between a set of selected industrial, demographic, and spatial variables, and individual city growth, during the decade 1951-1961.

Specifically, the rate of urban growth for 86 cities (Figure 7) for which data were available, was considered as a dependent variable. Twelve independent variables were selected on the expectation of a probable association with the dependent variable. These were as follows:

(1) Population size of city, 1951;

(2) Rate of urban population growth 1941-1951;

(3-4) Relative location to larger cities: distance to (a) nearest centers of one million and over, and (b) centers of 100,000 population and over;

Rate of change, 1951-1961, in

(5) Areal size of city;

(6) Male total labor force;

(7—11) Male labor force in each of the five nonagricultural categories;

(12) Male labor force in agriculture and related industries.[33]

Stepwise multiple regression was used for analysis; and as the value of many of the variables portrayed a highly skewed distribution, in order to better meet the assumptions of least-square regression, they were transformed to logarithmic form:

Highest r's: R^2 = .673
    Total labor force   .767
    Nonagricultural   .759
    Other services   .459

Significant variables were: change in total labor force, distance to nearest city of one million and over, and change in trade and commerce, nonagricultural employment, and in the areal size of the city. In addition to this more obvious growth response to employment change and areal change, an interesting inverse relation of relative growth to distance from the "million" cities was revealed. Even so, much of the variations in growth of cities remains to be explained.

URBAN-INDUSTRIAL DIMENSIONS OF STATES

In order to obtain a summary picture of the structure of urban industrial patterns in India, a factor analysis with 58 variables—demographic, industrial, cultural, and developmental—for 15 states was undertaken. (All the variables in the static and dynamic regression models for states were incorporated in this analysis.) The complex pattern of intercorrelation among the 58 variables revealed a smaller set of dimensions or independent ways in which the states of India vary. The results were useful in that urban places of differing sizes were revealed to behave in different ways.

DIMENSION 1: *Present status* (19½% of variance). Many closely related variables which measure the current economic development status of states constitute this strongest dimension: proportion of employment in the secondary sector has a .98 correlation (loading) on the factor; per capita income, .90; per capita electricity consumption, .89; and proportion of population urban, .86—especially in Class I centers .87, and Class II .79, respectively. The implication is that highly urban and metropolitan states with the best income are precisely those with the greatest existing industrialization and energy consumption.

DIMENSION 2: *Dynamism* (16½% of variance). Whatever the current status, states vary rather independently with respect to rate of growth. The variables contributing most strongly to the dimension include growth in nonagricultural employment, .90; growth in nonagricultural income, .89; of employment in manufacturing, .80, and in other services, .75.

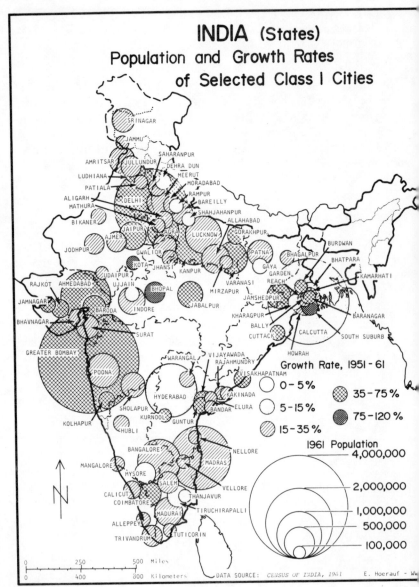

INDIA (States)
Population and Growth Rates
of Selected Class I Cities

Growth Rate, 1951-61
0 - 5%
5 - 15%
15 - 35%
35 - 75%
75 - 120%

1961 Population
4,000,000
2,000,000
1,000,000
500,000
100,000

0 250 500 Miles
0 400 800 Kilometers

DATA SOURCE: *CENSUS OF INDIA, 1961*   E. Hoerauf - WW

Figure 7.

DIMENSION 3: *Growth of medium-sized centers* (14% of variance). Dimension 1 relates to secondary sector and high status larger centers; dimension 2 relates to growth irrespective of urban size; dimension 3 reveals that the growth rate of medium-sized centers (Class III, .87), by states was independent of that for larger or smaller places and was most closely related to change in employment in transport, storage and communication, .91, and in other services, .78.

DIMENSION 4: *Smaller centers* (10% of variance). This dimension indicates that the situation of smallest centers (Class VI, .73) varies by states differently again, and is mostly related to change in construction employment, .92, and to some extent to migration, .60. This may not, however, be a very significant dimension, but a result of definitional variation.

DIMENSION 5: *Natural increase* (7% of variance). This dimension reveals that states vary by growth due to natural increase (.94) in a manner quite different than their rank on other characteristics. Other dimensions were of less significance, interest, or clarity.

SUMMARY

Static Models

The degree of urbanization in states was found to be very significantly related to the level of commercialization—that is, employment in the tertiary sector and number of retail and other establishments. Differences in the level of secondary employment did not seem to be as strongly reflected in differences in the degree of urbanization.

The proportion of the population of states residing in larger places (Classes I, II, III, IV) was fairly well related to the variables selected, and again, is largely a function of nonagricultural opportunities in general (or, as in case of the cities, a combination of the occupational, developmental, and cultural factors) rather than to secondary opportunities in particular. Commercial and service establishments, along with employment in the secondary sector and a high level of energy consumption, were most important to the Class I centers; a high level of per capita income, post offices, nonagricultural employment, and secondary sector to Class II centers; post offices, establishments, and nonagricultural employment to Class III centers; and secondary sector, natural increase of population, and transportational development (road) to Class IV centers.

Results for smaller centers (Classes V and VI) were less meaningful and additional variables would need to be found. Developmental variables such as hospitals and establishments were of some importance to the Class V centers; natural increase and migration, to the Class VI group.

In general, the level of urbanization is found to reflect the level of nonagricultural opportunities. Unfortunately, the kind of data available did not permit more basic analysis of why this level of nonagricultural opportunities varies across India. Such variables noted in the discussion of regression residuals—e.g., capital investment, resource levels, and availability of transport—would undoubtedly be important, as may be certain almost accidental developments of the colonial period.

Dynamic Models

With a few exceptions, the dynamic models were not too successful in accounting for change in the level of urbanization and urban growth over the decade. In general, the notion that investment in the secondary sector would lead to a greater degree of urban growth was not borne out, but rather urban growth was more associated with expansion of employment in services, transport, and trade. There was, however, a relation between income and prevalence of manufacturing; status, if not urban growth, seemed to be dependent on success in industrialization.

Results of the analysis of individual Class I centers indicated an association between urban growth and change in the total labor force and in the tertiary sector, as well as change in the city area, as expected. However, as in the preceding models, the hypothesis of a close relationship between city growth and occupational change in the secondary sector, particularly in manufacturing, was not supported.

A preliminary study on dimensions of states through factor analysis basically provided us with the same impression as derived from the regression models: that the secondary sector seems to have a definite association with the developmental status as reflected in the level of per capita income and energy consumption, but not with variations in urban growth or the level of urbanization in general.

CONCLUSION

As a consequence of our concern with the problems of urbanization in the developing nations, the primary focus of the present paper has been to explore the relationships between urbanization and selected demographic, socioeconomic, developmental, and spatial variables in India. It is felt that research on this aspect of relationships will be useful toward the formulation of a more realistic urban policy which is of paramount necessity in all developing countries. At the very least, it is hoped that preliminary investigations of this nature will stimulate further discussions and crosscultural research of processes leading to urban growth and development that have not been sufficiently studied in detail in the less-developed nations. However, we need to be careful in interpreting the outcome of the analyses not only because of limitation of data and inadequacy of models but, because our knowledge concerning the process of urbanization in a developing nation is far from complete. It is important to emphasize that in the present analyses, while noting the factors influencing urban growth and urbanization, we do not attach any firm causality to the relationship which may happen to exist among them, but rather prefer to recognize the following emerging patterns as urbanization tendencies:

(1) While the degree of urbanization of the states can be shown to be related to their level of commercialization in general (shops, commercial establishments, restaurants, theaters), and to the tertiary sector in particular, the proportion of population in some of the larger-size city classes appears to be moderately strongly related to a concomitant concentration of secondary employment.

(2) Percentage growth of urban population seems to be more a function of change in the tertiary sector than in the secondary, but neither provides a very complete explanation. The same pattern emerges in the analysis of urban growth in individual cities of over 100,000 population, where growth appears to be associated with change in total and nonagricultural labor force and employment in the tertiary, rather than the secondary, sector. The variables employed were particularly insufficient to account for statistical variations in urban growth in the various smaller size groups.

(3) Urbanization, or proportional change in urban population, appears to be more associated with total nonagricultural employment than either the secondary or tertiary sectors alone. However, clearly the more important variables explaining change in the level of urbanization have been left out in the present analysis; only size group III (20—50,000 population), possibly in consequence of the planning and developmental efforts directed toward the smaller centers, showed a sign of proportionate urban growth in direct relation to secondary and tertiary employment.

In view of the above general tendencies of urbanization, it appears that the notion of a close relationship between urbanization and the secondary sector in particular, or even the nonagricultural opportunities in general, is not significantly tenable in India, at least so far as the degree of urbanization and urban growth are concerned. Obviously, India's urban population has increased faster than employment in the secondary sector despite the tremendous industrial planning efforts launched by the government in recent years. This implies something of a self-generating growth in urban population, whatever the level of employment opportunities, and probably supports the idea of over-urbanization. Viewed in this light, however, the basic urbanization problem of India seems to be not so much one of where new opportunities are created, but of creating more of them. In spite of the fact that the rural-urban migration *rate* dropped in the 1951-1961 decade, the population-employment imbalance is partly explained by the huge *volume* of rural-urban migration, "due to excessively large growth of population in rural areas in relation to limited productivity" (Peach, 1968: 300), and partly due to a trend towards "capital intensive industrialization" (Ambannavar, 1970: 145).

The association of tertiary sector employment (indicating a broad expansion of commercial activities and services that, for want of a better word, we term as "tertiarization") with both the degree of urbanization and urban growth is not uncommon in the developing countries as well as in more developed ones. But, as many scholars have pointed out, while in the latter case this trend may signify a well-developed and mechanized primary and secondary sector along with a high standard of living, in the former situation it usually simply points toward a vast underemployed labor force. Even though the nature and role of tertiary activities in these nations, due to their "imperfect" occupational specialization, can be questioned, it is desirable that we note the dualistic nature of the tertiary employment structure in assessing its role in urbanization in India. This dualism is seen in the persistence of a highly skilled governmental and professional subsector on the one hand, and unskilled labor-intensive economic enterprises such as "services incidental" to transport, trade and commercial transactions on the other. The unorganized subsector, although characterized by "low productivity, underemployment, seasonal and casual" employment, is useful to the Indian urban dwellers whose values and styles of living, and hence some of their demands for certain goods and services, are still held in common with the rural living pattern.[34] Because these demands do not totally conform to the conventional urban pattern of life common in the developed nations, the providers of these wants are also likely to form a unique occupational structure. Thus, "tertiarization" in India—a pattern quite different from that in the Western models, and possibly similar, but not necessarily identical to, "tertiarism" as discussed in the context of other developing countries (Rios, 1971: 278)—should be explored to its fullest socio-economic implications on the study of urbanization and planning in the nation.

Many programs and policies have been proposed to address India's urban and regional problems. Among these, the all-out 'effort by the government of India to control population increase we consider to be the most crucial and important. This, along with other strategies that include containing the population in the rural areas or channeling them to the smaller urban centers through creation of job opportunities, modernization of the countryside, and dispersal of industries and services, are supposed to have the potential to reduce interregional as well as urban-rural disparities and imbalances. However the family planning efforts have not produced quite the hoped-for effects in the last decade, although the forthcoming census may prove otherwise, and we can only hope that India will experience a gradual reduction in the growth rate in the decades to come.

Furthermore, as has been painfully evident in the last few years, the various planning strategies, though perhaps wisely conceived and potentially workable, have turned out to be less than totally effective, primarily because of their piecemeal nature and nonintegrative approach, with the explosive issue of national versus regional or local planning still rampant among the scholars, laymen, and policymakers. "One of the criticisms of the planning procedure in India is that the country is still at the stage of 'project-planning,' rather than co-ordinated and integrated planning in all its aspects—economic, social and spatial—and at all levels—national, regional and local" (Vagale, 1968: 36). This is unfortunate. The emphasis should not be on one or the other, but on a well integrated urban and developmental policy. As Natarajan (1969: 27) has observed:

What is needed is a national policy for the economic development of regions guided by objectives for the organization of the national space economy. Planning based solely on sectoral allocations should hence forward seek to achieve the spatial co-ordination of sectoral programmes [see also Berry and Rao, 1968: 25].

The purpose of our research has not been to present any simplistic guideline to mitigate the complex problems of urbanization; more research and study are indeed needed before one can arrive at a realistic program. However, in light of the findings in the present study, it appears that a planning strategy aiming only at decentralization and relocation of industry from the larger to medium or smaller urban centers, if continued, would in itself have limited effect in relieving the nation's urban stress. Relocation of existing industries, indeed, would probably only aggravate the weakness of these urban economies.

"The regional planning problem for any Indian region," as Berry and Rao (1968: 29) have pointed out, "is that of replicating and administering a systematic process of industrial decentralization while continuing to center innovative, large scale, and capital-intensive activity in the country's largest metropoli" (see also Hoselitz, 1960a: 242). We concur with this view, but would emphasize that creation of job opportunities should be of prime consideration in planning. If in the few metropolises emphasis is placed on "capital-intensive" industrialization, in the rural areas and in the small and medium-sized urban centers, the policy of "labor-intensive" industries should be vigorously implemented. These industries need not necessarily be the "agro-industries" in the traditional sense, but may be viewed from a broader perspective that includes a wide array of industrial and commercial activities, creating "products and services" to satisfy the needs and rising demands of the people (Owens and Shaw, 1972: 112-113). This will not only create a broad employment base, but will also have the potential to bring about the much desired rural stability by reducing the so-called "rural push."

However, any effort toward improving the nation's urban environment ought to be based on a concrete knowledge of the existing and potential resources; strategies, plans, and policies are not likely to succeed, no matter how well-intentioned they are, if they are not based on a systematic appraisal of the relevant data and information.[35] To this effect, along with a concerted effort on the national and regional basis, integration and cooperation are also warranted from various disciplines equipped to contribute the findings in their respective fields toward a common cause. What we know now in the context of India's patterns is that any strategy which might emerge leaves ample scope for close collaboration of scholars from various fields of social sciences, not only from within the nation, but from across national boundaries. The benefits that can be accrued from such a coordinated approach are manifold: it would not only aid in viewing the problems more objectively, but the exchange of knowledge among international scholars would also help in understanding the process and patterns in different cultural settings and in devising potentially useful strategies to combat these problems.

NOTES

1. For selected examples, see Dasgupta (1971); Berry and Spodek (1971); Horton, McConnell, and Tirtha (1970); Berry and Rao (1968); Berry et al. (1966); and Ahmad (1965).

2. For an analytical discussion on the definition of urban places, see Asish Bose (1964); also Chandrasekaran and Zachariah (1964: 51-56).

3. For an extended discussion of these concepts, see for example, Otis Dudley Duncan (1957).

4. See for example, Unni (1965); Trivedi (1969); and Bhargava (1967).

5. For an explanation of the "scale of urbanization, see Gibbs (1966); for an application of this concept in India, see Mookherjee (1969).

6. For a lucid analysis of the apparent dichotomy of urban and rural life in India, see Chatterjee (1968).

7. Class I: those with population of 100,000 and above; Class II: with a population of 50,000-99,999; Class III: 20,000-49,999, Class IV: 10,000-19,999; Class V: 5,000-9,999; and Class VI: with less than 5,000 population. In the Indian census, as well as in the present study, only the Class I centers are referred to as "cities;" others are called "towns."

8. However, the inevitability of a "technical connection" between urbanization and industrialization has been questioned. See, as an example, Kuznets (1963: 102-103).

9. For example, Abu-Lughad (1965: 313) noted:

often one third or more of the urban labor force is employed in the tertiary (service) sector of the economy. Unlike countries of advanced industrialization, where such high rates reflect mechanization in the primary and secondary sectors, this allocation indicates that much of the unproductivity of urban workers is being concealed by a veil of often shoddy and marginal commercial enterprises of the "shoe-string" variety.

B. D. Sharma (1968: 487) observed:

It has also to be remembered that labour productivity does not increase in urban areas per se. The service sector is perhaps the most conspicuous and pervasive example of loosely organized, if not totally unorganized, type of economic activity. As Myrdal observes, "the distributive trade has long been a sponge for underutilized labor." We have a very large proportion of urban labor force in service occupation as compared to industrial occupations. In 1961, mining and manufacturing claimed 10.75% (in 1951, 10.25%) as against 20.12% (in 1951, 20.03%) for service industries.

10. For some viewpoints in this regard, see, for example, Mahajan (1965: 12) and Schwartzberg (1969: 228-229).

11. Also, the expediency of a clearcut distinction between secondary and tertiary sectors in the study of economic development and urbanization in the developing countries has been questioned. Higgins (1967: 119) for example, notes that "the cross-correlation between relative decline of the primary sector and relative growth of both secondary and tertiary sectors is so high that one can ignore the distinction between the secondary and tertiary sectors as a first approximation."

12. The 1971 census provisional figures reveal a continuous trend of urban concentration in the cities. While the urban population of 108,787,082 constitutes only 19.87% of the total population of India, 52.71% of this population load is borne by the Class I centers (*Census of India, 1971,* 1971: 5-6).

13. In terms of total labor force, a decline in the tertiary sector is noticeable; but, as noted in the census, male work force is considered as more "plausible and consistent" and therefore more reliable, as compared to the total labor force.

14. Regarding the possible reason behind this unique situation at Kerala, Basu (1965: 25) noted: "This suggests that many of the industries of this state have been established in big villages which have not yet been declared as urban."

15. However, as Beyer (1967: 320) has pointed out, "optimum city size for development has not been, and possibly cannot be definitively determined." For a brief discussion of the arguments for and against the optimal city size concept, see Wellisz (1971: 41-43).

16. In discussing the spread effect, Webber, noting Myrdal's view that due to the development of external diseconomies of scale, firms are forced to "look outside the growth poles for suitable locations," commented that "the growth of Megalopolis and of the London region reveal that external diseconomies may impinge only a little on firms' decisions" (1972: 80). The readiness of entrepreneurs to settle in the big cities, as is apparent from the licensing and establishment of industries in the private sector, lead us to share Webber's scepticism. However, as Lall and Tirtha (1971: 247) have noted:

> The tendency of an acceleration of growth in the medium sized towns, particularly after 1951 ... may be an indication of their increasing ability to attract some of the modern industrial and commercial activities at a time when the large cities, with their acute problems of congestion, suffer from several external diseconomies.

17. For a discussion of some of the problems and planning implications of the development of "new towns" see, Krishna Swami (1966-1967); see also Prakash (1969).

18. The exact population range for towns that may be called "medium" is subject to controversy; see, for example, Basu (1965: 29) and Harris (1959: 194). However, as Ram K. Vepa (1968: 494-495) has pointed out:

> the real criterion is not merely by the size of the population, but a number of other factors—such as availability of skilled personnel, credit facilities, proximity to market, access to raw materials, minimum facilities such as post and telegraph office, railroad, and general standing of the town in the life of the community. It would be possible to identify some such towns in each district, and ensure that all the necessary facilities are made available in the first instance to such towns so that they will develop as new growth centers. In most cases, they will be in the population range of 20,000 to 100,000 and will also be either Taluka or Block headquarters.

19. This point is discussed in an unpublished research paper by Mookherjee (1972).

20. For example, see Mandelkar (1961: 152). However, a "package programme" of this nature in Maharashtra did not fare too well; see Ram K. Vepa (1968: 492-493).

21. However, it should be noted that the Planning Commission, even during the first plan, was not totally unaware of the pitfalls of the industrial concentration in a "few select areas" and did acknowledge the need for establishment of industries in backward states and regions (Government of India, Planning Commission, 1953: 191).

22. For an excellent analysis of the recent policies on industrial location and urban growth, see Nath (1966); see also Roth (1970).

23. For a wide range of views on the nature, purpose, prospects, and problems of industrial estates in India, see, for example: De and Singha (1965); Raj (1965); Vagale (1967); and Vepa (1968: 494).

24. For a recommendation of vigorous governmental control in licensing new industrial establishments, see Lewis (1964: 197).

25. For a general discussion of developments in this context, see Thacker (1966: 40).

26. For example, in discussing "metropolitanization" in relation to industrialization, Wilkinson (1960) and Gibbs and Schnore (1960) used "workers in nonagricultural occupations" and "per capita energy consumption," respectively, as indicators of industrialization.

27. Gibbs and Schnore (1960; 160-170) provide a good example of this.

28. Asish Bose (1965: 2) noted:

In the 1951 Census, livelihood class V, Production other than Cultivation lumped together all workers in different types of industries, household, cottage, small and large, and there was no way of knowing the exact size of the working force engaged in the modern manufacturing sector. In the 1961 Census, livelihood class V of the 1951 Census was split into Industrial Categories III, IV and V, and Category V was restricted to workers in manufacturing industries only (other than household industries). This greatly facilitates a study of working force in the manufacturing sector. In some of our tables, however, Industrial Categories IV and V of the 1961 census have been lumped together for making them comparable with 1951 census figures.

29. One example of the minor but rather exasperating inconsistencies of census data is the discrepancy between the figures for the total population in each state for 1951 in two places in the same volume (*Census of India, 1961,* 1962: 8-9 versus 402).

30. Here we support the proposals to create an urban data bank with international scope and organization that would facilitate research and exchange of information and ideas. For a lucid discussion on the concept and potential use of data banks, see Moyer (1971); for some general guidelines on "Urban Information Systems," see National Research Council (1969: 65-76).

31. An excellent discussion on the "properties, uses and objectives" of the maps of residuals from regression can be seen in Edwin N. Thomas (1968).

32. This section is an excerpt from a research paper by Mookherjee and Morrill (1972).

33. Labor force in agriculture and related activities consists of workers as cultivator; as agricultural laborer; in mining, quarrying, livestock, forestry, fishing, hunting and plantations, orchards, and allied activities. For details see (*Census of India, 1961,* 1962: 3).

34. The prevalence of using cowdung cakes as cooking fuel, even in the urban areas, to offer just one example, has created a unique occupation for a number of people, whose major income is derived from the making and hawking of these cakes.

35. We must beware of the lures of vague theorizations without a sound foundation of information derived from rigorous research. As A. Bose (1971: 81) has pointed out:

Flimsy generalizations like "over-urbanization of Asian countries," superficial analyses of "push and pull" factors affecting migration, and platitudinous prescriptions like "balanced and integrated" development of urban and rural areas, to give just a few examples, confuse the issues instead of clarifying them. In the developing countries of Asia, there is need for much more data on migration and urbanization, but the greatest need is for a realistic appraisal of the Asian scene, and a clear understanding of Asian problems in an Asian setting.

This comment, though a little too harsh, and perhaps not totally justified, nevertheless indicates the necessity for more empirical studies in Asia today.

REFERENCES

ABU-LUGHAD, J. L. (1965) "Urbanization in Egypt: present state and future prospect." Econ. Development and Cultural Change 13 (April): 313-343.

AHMAD, Q. (1965) Indian Cities: Characteristics and Correlates. University of Chicago, Department of Geography, Research Paper 102.

AMBANNAVAR, J. P. (1970) "Change in the employment pattern of the Indian working force." Developing Economies 8 (March): 128-146.

ANDERSON, N. (1959) The Urban Community. New York: Henry Holt.

ASTHANA, B. N. and S. S. SRIVASTAVA (1965) Applied Statistics of India. Allahabad: Chaitanya.

BASU, D. D. (1965) "Industrialization as a factor influencing urban and regional development." J. of the Institute of Town Planners, Nos. 42 and 43 (March-June): 24-30.

BAUER, P. T. and Y. S. YAMI (1954) "Further notes on economic progress and occupational distribution." Econ. J. 64 (March): 98-106.

BAUER, P. T. and Y. S. YAMI (1951) "Economic progress and occupational distribution." Econ. J. 61 (December): 741-755.

BERRY, B.J.L. (1966) Essays on Commodity Flows and the Spatial Structure of the Indian Economy. University of Chicago, Department of Geography, Research Paper 111.

――― and V.L.S. P. RAO (1968) "Urban-rural duality in the regional structure of Andhra Pradesh: a challenge to regional planning and development." Geographische Zeitschrift No. 21.

BERRY, B.J.L. and H. SPODEK (1971) "Comparative ecologies of large Indian cities." Econ. Geography 47 (June): 266-285.

BEYER, G. H. (1967) "Resume: themes and issues," pp. 302-335 in G. H. Beyer (ed.) The Urban Explosion in Latin America. Ithaca, N.Y.: Cornell Univ. Press.

BHARGAVA, G. (1967) "Rurban dimensional planning for India." Khadigramodyog 13 (February): 373-387.

BOSE, A. (1971) "The urbanization process in South and Southeast Asia," pp. 81-109 in L. Jakobson and V. Prakash (eds.) Urbanization and National Development. Beverly Hills: Sage Pubns.

――― (1968) "Urban characteristics of towns in India: a statistical study." Indian J. of Public Administration [special number] 14 (July-September): 457-465.

――― (1965) Aspects of Working Force in India. New Delhi: Shri Ram Center Press.

――― (1964) "A note on the definition of 'town' in the Indian census: 1901-1961." Indian Econ. and Social Review (January-March): 84-94.

――― (1961) "Population growth and the industrialization-urbanization process in India." Man in India 41 (October-December): 255-275.

[67]

BOSE, D. K. (1969) "Urbanization, industrialization and planning for regional development." Econ. and Pol. Weekly, No. 4 (July): 1169-1172.

BROWNING, H. L. (1967) "Urbanization and modernization in Latin America: the demographic perspective," pp. 71-116 in G. H. Beyer (ed.) The Urban Explosion in Latin America. Ithaca, N.Y.: Cornell Univ. Press.

BURTON, I. (1969) "Natural resource planning: theory and practice," pp. 149-183 in M. M. Hufschmidt (ed.) Regional Planning: Challenge and Prospects. New York: Praeger.

Census of India, 1971 (1971) "Paper 1 of 1971–Supplement, Provisional Population Totals." Delhi: Office of the Registrar General and Census Commissioner.

Census of India, 1961 (1968) "Paper No. 1 of 1967, Subsidiary Tables B-I.6." Delhi: Office of the Registrar General and Census Commissioner.

––– (1967) "Electricity supply in India: an analysis of power and development during the two five year plan periods, 1951-1956 and 1956-1961." Delhi: Ministry of Home Affairs, Office of the Registrar General, Monograph No. 6.

––– (1964a) Vol. 1, Part II-A(i), "Population Table." Delhi: Office of the Registrar General and Census Commissioner.

––– (1964b) Vol. 1, Part II-B(i), "General Economic Tables." Delhi: Office of the Registrar General and Census Commissioner.

––– (1964c) Vol. 1, Part II-C(i). Delhi: Office of the Registrar General and Census Commissioner.

––– (1962) "Paper No. 1 of 1962. Final Population Tables." Delhi: Office of the Registrar General and Census Commissioner.

––– (1962) "Paper No. 1 of 1962. Final Population Tables." Delhi: Ministry of Home Affairs, Office of the Registrar General and Census Commissioner.

Central Statistical Organization (1963-1964) Statistical Abstract of the Indian Union, 1963 and 1964. Delhi: Cabinet Secretariat, Department of Statistics.

CHANDRASEKARAN, C. and K. C. ZACHARIAH (1964) "Concepts used in defining urban population and data available on its characteristics in countries of Southern Asia," pp. 51-70 in UNESCO, Urban-Rural Differences in Southern Asia; Report on Regional Seminar, Delhi, 1962. Delhi: UNESCO Research Centre on Social and Economic Development in Southern Asia.

CHATTERJEE, M. (1968) "The town/village dichotomy in India." Man in India 48 (July-September): 193-200.

COLM, G. and T. GEIGER (1962) "Country programming as a guide to development," pp. 45-70 in Development of the Emerging Countries: An Agenda for Research. Washington, D.C.: Brookings Institution.

CRANE, R. (1955) "Urbanism in India." Amer. J. of Sociology 60 (March): 463-470.

DASGUPTA, B. (1971) "Socio-economic classification of districts: a statistical approach." Econ. and Pol. Weekly 6 (August 14): 1763-1774.

DAVIS, K. (1951) The Population of India and Pakistan. Princeton: Princeton Univ. Press.

––– and H. H. GOLDEN (1957) "Urbanization and the development of pre-industrial areas," pp. 120-140 in P. K. Hatt and A. J. Reiss, Jr. (eds.) Cities and Society. Glencoe, Ill.: Free Press.

DE, A. K. and K. C. SINGHA (1965) "Industrial estates–their historical background and planning proposals." J. of the Institute of Town Planners, Nos. 42 and 43 (March-June): 58-61.

DESAI, P. B. (1968) "Economy of Indian cities." Indian J. of Public Administration 14 (July-September): 449-456.

DUNCAN, O. D. (1957) "Community size and the rural-urban continuum," pp. 35-45 in P. K. Hatt and A. J. Reiss, Jr. (eds.) Cities and Society. Glencoe, Ill.: Free Press.

FISHER, A.G.B. (1952) "A note on tertiary production." Econ. J. 62 (December): 820-834.

FRIEDMANN, J. and T. LACKINGTON (1967) "Hyperurbanization and national development in Chile: some hypotheses." Urban Affairs Q. 11 (June): 3-29.

GIBBS, J. P. (1966) "Measures of urbanization," Social Forces 45 (December): 170-177.

——— (1961) Urban Research Methods. New York: D. Van Nostrand.

——— and W. T. MARTIN (1962) "Urbanization, technology, and the division of labor: international patterns." Amer. Soc. Rev. 27 (October): 667-677.

GIBBS, J. P. and L. F. SCHNORE (1960) "Metropolitan growth: an international study." Amer. J. of Sociology 66 (September): 160-170.

GLASS, R. (1964) "Introduction and conclusions," pp. 1-29 in UNESCO, Urban-Rural Differences in Southern Asia; Report on Regional Seminar, Delhi, 1962. Delhi: UNESCO Research Centre on Social and Economic Development in Southern Asia.

GOLDEN, H. H. (1955) "Literary and social change in underdeveloped countries." Rural Sociology 20 (March): 1-7.

GOSAL, C. S. (1964) "Literacy in India: an interpretative study." Rural Sociology 29 (September): 261-277.

Government of India, Planning Commission (1953) The First Five Year Plan. Delhi: Government of India Press.

HAM, E. (1973) "Urbanization and Asian lifestyles," Annals 405 (January): 104-113.

HANNA, W. J. and J. L. HANNA (1971) Urban Dynamics in Black Africa. Chicago: Aldine-Atherton.

HARRIS, B. (1962) "Urban centralization and planned development," pp. 261-276 in R. Turner (ed.) India's Urban Future. Berkeley and Los Angeles: Univ. of California Press.

——— (1959) "Urbanization policy in India." Papers and Proceedings of the Regional Sci. Assn. 5: 181-203.

HAUSER, P. M. (1959) "Demographic indicators of economic development." Econ. Development and Cultural Change 7 (January): 98-116.

——— (1957) "Summary report of the general rapporteur," pp. 3-32 in P. M. Hauser (ed.) Urbanization in Asia and the Far East. Calcutta: UNESCO Research Centre on the Social Implications of Industrialization in Southern Asia.

HEBERLE, R. (1948) "Social consequences of the industrialization of southern cities." Social Forces 27 (October): 29-37.

HIGGINS, B. (1967) "The city and economic development," pp. 117-174 in G. H. Beyer (ed.) Urban Explosion in Latin America. Ithaca, N.Y.: Cornell Univ. Press.

HORTON, F. E., H. McCONNELL, and R. TIRTHA (1970) "Spatial patterns of socio-economic structure in India." Tijdschrift voor Economische en Sociale Geografie 61 (March-April): 101-113.

HOSELITZ, B. F. (1960a) Sociological Aspects of Economic Growth. New York: Free Press.

——— (1960b) "Urbanization in India." Kyklos 13 (June): 361-372.

——— (1957) "Urbanization and economic growth in Asia." Econ. Development and Cultural Change 6 (October): 42-54.

JAKOBSON, L. and V. PRAKASH (1971) "Urbanization and urban development," pp. 15-38 in L. Jakobson and V. Prakash (eds.) Urbanization and National Development. Beverly Hills: Sage Pubns.

KAMERSCHEN, D. R. (1969) "Further analysis of overurbanization." Econ. Development and Cultural Change 17 (January): 235-253.

——— (1968) "Literacy and socioeconomic development." Rural Sociology 33 (June): 175-188.

KHURANA, S. C. (1965) "Urbanization in India—a case for satellite towns." J. of the Institute of Town Planners, Nos. 42 and 43 (March-June): 15-21.

KRISHNA SWAMI, M. C. (1966-1967) "New towns in India: town development problems and implications." J. of the Institute of Town Planners, Nos. 49-50 (December-March): 40-51.

KUZNETS, S. (1963) "Consumption, industrialization and urbanization," pp. 99-115 in B. F. Hoselitz and W. E. Moore (eds.) Industrialization and Society. New York: UNESCO-Morton.

LALL, A. and R. TIRTHA (1971) "Spatial analysis of urbanization in India." Tijdschrift voor Economische en Sociale Geografie 62 (July-August): 234-247.

LAMPARD, E. E. (1965) "Historical aspects of urbanization," pp. 519-554 in P. M. Hauser and L. F. Schnore (eds.) The Study of Urbanization. New York: John Wiley.

LEWIS, J. P. (1964) Quiet Crisis in India. Washington, D. C.: Brookings Institution.

MAHAJAN, O. P. (1965) "1961 census—a study in regional economic disparities." Indian Econ. Assn. Papers (December 29-31): 11-21.

MANDELKAR, M. R. (1961) "Locational aspects of industries in Maharashtra state," pp. 151-154 in Problems of Starting an Industrial Enterprise. Report of a Seminar Organized by the Indian Institute of Public Administration, Bombay Regional Branch.

MATHAI, P. M. (1965) "Growth centers." Khadigramodyog 11 (May): 591-593.

MEHTA, S. (1961) "A comparative analysis of the industrial structure of the urban labor force of Burma and the United States." Econ. Development and Cultural Change 9 (January): 164-179.

MOOKHERJEE, D. (1972) "Cities and towns of India: ecological patterns and implications for policy formulation." [mimeo]

——— (1969) "Urbanization pattern in India: 1951-1961." Professional Geographer 21 (September): 308-314.

——— and R. L. MORRILL (1972) "Growth of Indian Cities." [mimeo]

MOYER, D. D. (1971) "Data banks." Plan Canada [special issue] (May): 57-65.

MUKHERJEE, R. (1963) "Urbanization and social transformation in India." Internatl. J. of Compar. Sociology 4 (September): 178-210.

MURPHY, R. (1972) "City and countryside as ideological issues: India and China." Compar. Studies in Society and History 14 (June): 250-267.

NAMBOODIRI, N. K. (1966) "A contribution to the study of within-urban and within rural differentials." Rural Sociology 31 (March): 29-39.

NATARAJAN, B. (1968) "Regional planning in its relation to national planning." J. of the Institute of Town Planners (June-September): 25-32.

NATH, V. (1966) "Planning for urban growth." Indian J. of Social Work 27 (July): 119-145.

National Council of Applied Economic Research (1967) Estimates of State Income. New Delhi.

National Research Council (1969) A Strategic Approach to Urban Research and Development: Social and Behavioral Science Considerations. Report of the Committee on Social and Behavior Urban Research, Division of Behavioral Sciences, to the U.S. Department of Housing and Urban Development.

OWENS, E. and R. SHAW (1972) Development Reconsidered. Lexington: D. C. Heath.

PEACH, G.C.K. (1968) "Urbanization in India," pp. 297-303 in R. P. Beckindale and J. M. Houston (eds.) Urbanization and Its Problems. Oxford: Basil Blackwell.

PRAKASH, V. (1969) New Towns in India. Charlotte, N.C.: Duke University Program in Comparative Studies on Southern Asia, Monograph 8.

RAJ, D. (1969) "The machinery for regional planning and development," pp. 301-310 in P. B. Desai, I. M. Grossack, and K. N. Sharma (eds.) Regional Perspective of Industrial and Urban Growth: The Case of Kanpur. Bombay: MacMillan Ltd.

RAJ, S. D. (1965) "Industrial estates: an appraisal of policies and programmes." J. of the Institute of Town Planners, Nos. 42 and 43 (March-June): 66-75.

RIOS, J. A. (1971) "The growth of cities and urban development," pp. 269-288 in J. Saunders (ed.) Modern Brazil: New Patterns and Development. Gainesville: Univ. of Florida Press.

RIVKIN, M. D. (1967) "Urbanization and national development: some approaches to the dilemma." Socio-Econ. Planning Sciences 1 (December): 117-142.

ROTH, I. (1970) "Industrial location and Indian government policy." Asian Survey 10 (May): 383-396.

ROTTENBERG, S. (1953) "Note on economic progress and occupational distribution." Rev. of Economics and Statistics 35 (May): 168-170.

SCHNORE, L. F. (1963) "The statistical measurement of urbanization and economic development." Land Economics 27 (August): 229-245.

SCHWARTZBERG, J. E. (1969) Occupational Structure and Level of Economic Development in India: A Regional Analysis. Delhi: Census of India, 1961, Monograph 4.

SEN GUPTA, P. and G. SDASYUK (1968) Economic Regionalization of India: Problems and Approaches. Delhi: Census of India, 1961, Monograph 8.

SHARMA, B. D. (1968) "Urbanization and economic development." Indian J. of Public Administration 14 (July-September): 474-490.

SJOBERG, G. (1965) "Cities in developing and in industrial societies: a cross-cultural analysis," pp. 213-263 in P. M. Hauser and L. F. Schnore (eds.) The Study of Urbanization. New York: John Wiley.

SOVANI, N. V. (1966) Urbanization and Urban India. New York: Asia Publishing House.

STOCKWELL, E. G. (1966) "Some demographic correlates of economic development." Rural Sociology 31 (June): 216-224.

STONER, G. E., Jr. (1965) "Notable geographical contribution of the Indian census of 1961." Professional Geographer 17 (November): 17-20.

THACKER, M. S. (1965) India's Urban Problem. Mysore: Univ. of Mysore.

THOMAS, E. N. (1968) "Maps of residuals from regression," pp. 326-352 in B.J.L. Berry and D. F. Marble (eds.) Spatial Analysis: a Reader in Statistical Geography. Englewood Cliffs, N.J.: Prentice-Hall, Inc.

TRIVEDI, H. R. (1969) "The 'semi-urban pocket' as concept and reality in India." Human Organization 28 (Spring): 72-77.

UNESCO, (1964) "Is there a rural-urban dichotomy?" pp. 39-43 in UNESCO, Urban Rural Differences in Southern Asia; Report on Regional Seminar Delhi, 1962. Delhi: UNESCO Research Centre on Social and Economic Development in Southern Asia.

UNNI, K. R. (1965) "Rurban villages." J. of the Institute of Town Planners, Nos. 42 and 43 (March-June): 163-166.

VAGALE, L. R. (1968) "National development planning in its relation to urban and regional planning." J. of the Institute of Town Planners, Nos. 55-56 (June-September): 33-37.

––– (1967) "A note on the layout of industrial estates in India." J. of the Institute of Town Planners, No. 52 (September): 34-37.

––– (1965) "Indian cities and industries: impacts and relationships." J. of the Institute of Town Planners, Nos. 42-43 (March-June): 31-42.

VEPA R. K. (1968) "Urbanization and industrial development." Indian J. of Public Administration 14 (July-September): 490-497.

WARD, B. (1969) "The poor world's cities." Economist (December 6-12): 56-70.

WEBBER, M. J. (1972) Impact of Uncertainty on Location. Cambridge, Mass.: M.I.T. Press.

WELLER, R. H. and D. F. SLY (1969) "Modernization and demographic change: a world view." Rural Sociology 34 (September): 313-326.

WELLISZ, S. H. (1971) "Economic development and urbanization," pp. 39-55 in L. Jakobson and V. Prakash (eds.) Urbanization and National Development. Beverly Hills: Sage Pubns.

WILKINSON, T. O. (1960) "Urban structure and industrialization." Amer. Soc. Rev. 25 (June): 356-363.

WIRTH, L. (1957) "Urbanism as a way of life," pp. 46-63 in P. K. Hatt and A. J. Reiss, Jr. (eds.) Cities and Society. Glencoe, Ill.: Free Press.

YADAVA, J. S. (1970) "Urbanization and peasant culture: a case study." Asian Studies 8 (December): 301-306.

APPENDIX

NATURE AND SOURCE OF DATA

Model 1 (a, b)

URBAN: Total urban population and that of each urban class size, I through VI, as percentage of state total population, 1961 [urban population: *Census of India, 1961* (1964a: 272-274); state total population: *Census of India, 1961* (1962: 8-9)].

INDUSTRIAL: Male workers in each of the following nonagricultural industrial categories as percentage of the state total population: household and manufacturing; construction; trade and commerce; transport, storage and communication; and other services, 1961 [*Census of India, 1961* (1962: 408-409); for details regarding the nature of each of these categories, see *Census of India, 1961* (1964b: 1-4)].

LITERACY: Literates per thousand state total population, 1961 [*Census of India, 1961* (1964c: 94)].

EDUCATIONAL INSTITUTIONS: Recognized educational institutions per thousand state total population, 1961. "Recognized Institutions are those which are recognized by the Government or by a University or a Board of Secondary and Intermediate Education, constituted by law and offer the prescribed courses of study.... Only those research institutions are taken which provide facilities for teaching" [Central Statistical Organization (1963-1964: 598); see pp. 590-598 and 586 for details regarding the nature of various institutions that belong to this category].

SCHOLARS IN RECOGNIZED INSTITUTIONS: Men and women receiving instruction in various stages of general education and in various subjects of professional and special education as percentage of state total population, 1961 [Central Statistical Organization (1963-1964: 605); for details, see pp. 586-587, 599-605].

MOTOR VEHICLES: Number of motor vehicles taxed during the last quarter (ending March) of 1961, per thousand state total population. This category includes motorcycles, auto rickshaws, jeeps, private cars, public service vehicles (motor, cabs, others), goods vehicles, and miscellaneous. "The figures . . . may be taken to represent the bulk of the serviceable vehicles" [Central Statistical Organization (1963-1964: 342, 344)].

ESTABLISHMENTS (covered by the Shops and Commercial Establishments Acts): Shops; commercial establishments; and restaurants and theaters per thousand state total population, 1961 (1962 for Manipur) [Central Statistical Organization (1963-1964: 533); for details, see p. 478].

POST OFFICES: Permanent post offices, 1961-1962, per thousand state total population [Central Statistical Organization (1963-1964: 385)].

HOSPITALS: Hospitals per ten thousand state total population, 1961 [Central Statistical Organization (1963-1964: 563)].

SURFACED ROAD: Extra-municipal ("roads outside the area or jurisdiction of a Municipality, Town or City Corporation or other urban body"); surfaced roads per ten thousand state total population, 1961 [Central Statistical Organization (1963-1964: 354); for details, see pp. 349-350].

ELECTRICITY: Annual per capita consumption of electricity, 1961 [*Census of India, 1961* (1967: 59)].

PER CAPITA INCOME: [National Council of Applied Economic Research (1967: 57)].

PERCENTAGE NET VARIATION IN POPULATION, 1951-1961.

PERCENTAGE NET INCREASE/DECREASE BY INTERNAL MIGRATION AND IMMIGRATION, 1951-1961.

PERCENTAGE OF NATURAL INCREASE OF POPULATION, 1951-1961: [Sen Gupta and Sdasyuk (1968: 87)].

Model 2 (a, b, c)

Variables in 2-a are expressed as percentage variations—i.e., the difference between 1961 and 1951 as percentage of the base in 1951. The urban and industrial variables in 2-b are calculated as change in the percentage of urban population or industrial workers to state population total, 1951-1961. The remaining variables are the same as in 2-a. The industrial variables in 2-c are expressed as change in the percentage of industrial workers to total male workers instead of the state population total, as in 2-b. In all other aspects this model is identical to 2-b.

URBAN (all variables): [urban population: *Census of India, 1961* (1964a: 272-274); state total population: *Census of India, 1961* (1962: 402)]. (Even though they are in the same census volume—namely, *Census of India, 1961* (1962)—the data on state total population for 1951 on pp. 8-9 and on p. 402 do not tally. However, the data for 1961 on pp. 8-9 and on pp. 408-409 are the same. Consequently, for the sake of uniformity, the state population data in Model 2 are taken from pp. 402 and 408-409, instead of pp. 8-9 as in Model 1.)

INDUSTRIAL (all variables): [*Census of India, 1961* (1962: 402, 408-409) for all states except Maharashtra and Gujarat, 1951; for these states, 1951: *Census of India, 1961* (1968: 7-12)].

STATE INCOME: Percentage variation on state income in the following nonagricultural sectors: mining, manufacturing and construction; trade and commerce; transport, storage and communications; all other services including house property [National Council of Applied Economic Research (1967: 65-71)].

NET DOMESTIC PRODUCT: Change in the statewide percentage distribution of net domestic product by the following economic sectors: manufacturing industries; trade and commerce; transport, storage and communication; and other services [National Council of Applied Economic Research (1967: 60, 62)].

PER CAPITA INCOME: [National Council of Applied Economic Research (1967: 58)].

ELECTRICITY: Annual per capita consumption of electricity, 1951-1961 [*Census of India, 1961* (1967: 59). For data on annual per capita consumption of electricity in 1951, that of Hyderabad (1951) has been used for Andhra Pradesh (1951); that of Bombay State (1951) has been used for Gujarat (1951) and Maharashtra (1951); and that of Travancore-Cochin (1951) has been used for Kerala (1951)].

PERCENTAGE NET VARIATION IN POPULATION,1951-1961.

PERCENTAGE NET INCREASE/DECREASE BY INTERNAL MIGRATION AND EMIGRATION 1951-1961.

PERCENTAGE OF NATURAL INCREASE OF POPULATION, 1951-1961: [Sen Gupta and Sdasyuk (1968: 87)].

City Growth

URBAN (all variables): [*Census of India, 1961* (1964a: 363-400)].
INDUSTRIAL (all variables): [*Census of India, 1961* (1968: 41-100)].
CITY AREA: [*Census of India, 1961* (1964a: 120-128, 363-400)].
ROAD DISTANCE: [Calculated from maps].

DEBNATH MOOKHERJEE is currently professor of Geography and Director of Urban and Regional Planning Program at Western Washington State College. He holds a Ph.D. in Geography from the University of Florida. His major fields of interest are urbanization and regional development, and he has contributed a number of articles and papers to various professional journals and at international conferences. The present volume is an outcome of a research project he initiated during his residence as a visiting scholar at the University of Washington while on sabbatical leave from W.W.S.C. during the 1969-1970 academic year.

RICHARD L. MORRILL is presently Professor of Geography and Chairman of the department at the University of Washington, where he received his Ph.D. degree. His areas of interests are social geography and quantitative methods. He has authored numerous articles, and his most recent books are: The Spatial Organizaton of Society *(1970) and* The Geography of Poverty in the United States *(with E. H. Wohlenburg, 1971).*

Better Way of
etting New Information

earch, survey and policy studies that say what needs to be said—
more, no less.

Sage Papers Program

regularly-issued original paperback series that bring, at an unusually
cost, the timely writings and findings of the international scholarly
munity. Since the material is updated on a continuing basis, each
s rapidly becomes a unique repository of vital information.

horitative, and frequently seminal, works that NEED to be available

- To scholars and practitioners
- In university and institutional libraries
- In departmental collections
- For classroom adoption

Professional Papers

PARATIVE POLITICS SERIES
ERNATIONAL STUDIES SERIES
MINISTRATIVE AND POLICY STUDIES SERIES
ERICAN POLITICS SERIES

Policy Papers

WASHINGTON PAPERS

SAGE PUBLICATIONS
The Publishers of Professional Social Science
Beverly Hills • London

Sage Professional Papers in **Comparative Politics**

Editors: Harry Eckstein, *Princeton University,* Ted Robert Gurr, *Northwestern University,* and Aristide R. Zolberg, *University of Chicago.*

ORDER FORM

_____
name

_____
institution

_____
address

_____
city/state/zip

Please enter subscription(s) to:

☐ Prof. Pprs. in Administrative & Policy Studies

☐ Prof. Pprs. in Comparative Politics

☐ Prof. Pprs. in American Politics

☐ Prof. Pprs. in International Studies

☐ The Washington Papers

Please send the individual papers whose numbers I have listed below:

_____

_____

_____

☐ Please invoice (INSTITUTIONS ONLY) quot-
ing P.O. # _____(shipping and
handling additional on non-subscription orders)

☐ Payment enclosed (Sage pays shipping charges)

INSTITUTIONAL ORDERS FOR LESS THAN $10.00 AND _ALL_ PERSONAL ORDERS _MUST BE PREPAID_. (California residents: please add 6% sales tax on non-subscription orders.)

MAIL TO:

 SAGE Publications, Inc. / P.O. Box 5024 Beverly Hills, California 90210

orders from the U.K., Europe, the Middle East and Africa should be sent to Sage Publications, Ltd, 44 Hatton Garden, London EC1N 8ER

SAGE PROFESSIONAL PAPERS
■ ■ ■ GENERAL INFORMATION FOR ALL FOUR SERIES

These series are designed with both research and classroom usage in mind; papers are available either on subscription (assuring quick receipt of timely work in the field – as well as savings that average between 50% and 60% off the regular single copy prices) or as single titles for personal or classroom use (priced at $2.00 to $3.00 each, depending on length). Papers range in length from 32 to 96 pages; articles are published which are too long for normal journal publication, yet too short to become books.

Frequency: twelve papers per year in each series, published in groups of four throughout the year.

Paper Edition, Unbound – Subscription Rates (for each series)

	Institutional	*Individual*
One year	$21.00/£8.00	$12.00/£5.40
Two years	$41.00/£15.50	$23.00/£10.40
Three years	$60.00/£23.00	$33.00/£15.40

Outside the U.S. and Canada, add $2.00 per year to above rates.

Subscription discounts to professionals and students are granted ONLY on orders paid by personal check or money order. Wherever possible, payment should accompany orders, since service will not begin until payment has been received.

Bound Library Edition Available in three clothbound parts (each containing four papers) per year (in each series).
Subscription Price $30.00/£12.00 per year (i.e., $10.00/£4.00 per bound part) for each series.
Regular Price $37.50/£18.75 per annual volume (i.e., $12.50/£6.25 per bound part) – if bound parts are ordered separately, or after publication.
Outside the U.S. and Canada, add $2.00 per volume (or $.75 per part) to the above rates.

What is a SAGE PROFESSIONAL PAPER?

According to CHOICE (a magazine of the American Library Association) — when reviewing our series of professional papers in comparative politics — it's a "most valuable, inexpensive . . . outlet for research products" which provides "specialists with high quality monographs too narrow and short to appear as full-length books and rather too long to be published in academic journals . . . An extremely useful library acquisition."
ASK YOUR LIBRARIAN TO ORDER *ALL* THESE IMPORTANT SERIES TODAY !!!